THE STORY OF
DURHAM

THE STORY OF
DURHAM

DOUGLAS POCOCK

To Gilly

First published 2013

The History Press
The Mill, Brimscombe Port
Stroud, Gloucestershire, GL5 2QG
www.thehistorypress.co.uk

British Library Cataloguing in Publication Data.
A catalogue record for this book is available from the British Library.

ISBN 978 0 7524 9978 9

Typesetting and origination by The History Press
Printed in Great Britain

CONTENTS

INTRODUCTION AND ACKNOWLEDGEMENTS

This is the story of a city that medieval writers likened to Jerusalem, which Ruskin termed one of the wonders of the world, and which Pevsner more modestly called one of the architectural experiences of Europe. As the narrator, I write out of four decades of acquaintance with the city in which I have been privileged to live and work. During this period, appreciation has deepened, as the inquisitiveness of an incomer matured into a deeper form of engagement and caring. To the initial attraction of the physical form was given social significance and spiritual meaning.

In the process of becoming acquainted, I acknowledge the contribution of my friends and colleagues in the University and City of Durham Trust, the local civic amenity society. Above all I acknowledge the role of my life's companion, Gillian, dispenser of encouragement, wisdom and common sense.

In compiling this volume I benefited particularly from the encyclopaedic knowledge of Roger Norris and the vast photographic collection of Gilesgate Archives, which Michael Richardson generously put at my disposal. I should also like to express my gratitude to the kindness afforded by Richard Brickstock, David Butler, Philip Davies, Norman Emery, the librarians of Clayport Library, Chris Orton, who professionally produced many of the maps, and Dennis and Jo Jones, who proofread and commented on much of the manuscript.

I acknowledge with gratitude the permission granted by the following persons and institutions to publish the following illustrations. (An asterisk alongside a few maps indicates a partial 'borrowing'.)

Gilesgate Archive: 5, 22, 50, 53, 56, 57, 61, 62, 64a, 64c, 66, 67, 68, 69, 70, 74, 76, 81, 82, 83a, 85, 86, 87, 88, 89, 91, 96. Durham County Council: 16, 32*, 75. Chapter of Durham Cathedral: 11, 34, 35, 43, 80, 83a, 84. Durham University Library: 24, 37. Durham Castle Museum: 10, 21, 36, 72, 73. Archaeology Department, University of Durham: 3*, 4*, 6*, 29*. The Architectural Press: 90. British Association for the Advancement of Science:

59, 60. The British Library: 40. Harrison and Harrison: 64b. The National Galleries of Scotland, Edinburgh: 112. The *Northern Echo*: 83c. NRM/Science and Society Picture Library: 8. Philatelic Bureau, Edinburgh: 98. Society of Antiquities of London: 14a. Margaret Bonney: 3*, 30*. Dae Sasitorn/lastrefuge.co.uk: 2. Martin Leyland: 9. John Pounder: 39. Martin Roberts: 33. Royston Thomas: 124. Malcolm Thurlby: 12, 13. The following photographs by the author are reproduced by the courtesy of the Chapter of Durham Cathedral: 17, 18, 19, 25, 26, 27, 28. Figure 90 is from Thomas Sharp, *Cathedral City: A Plan for Durham City*, The Architectural Press, London (1945) and Figure 92 is from Frederick Gibberd, *Town Design*, The Architectural Press (1959), both copyright John Wiley & Co. Ltd and reproduced with permission. The quotations from the poems, 'Going, going', by Philip Larkin, from *Collected Poems by Philip Larkin* (1988) and 'Four Quartets' by T.S. Eliot, from *Collected Poems 1909–1962* by T.S. Eliot (1963) are reproduced by kind permission of Faber and Faber Ltd. Shepherds Dene Retreat House, Riding Mill, Northumberland for W.R. Robinson, *Durham*, (1846), detail, on the front cover.

one

BEGINNINGS

The Physical Setting

The story of Durham, no less than the visual drama of the city, is integrally related to its physical setting. A rolling topography, which encouraged medieval travellers to perceive seven hills, as befits a holy city, may to the more discerning, if less romantic, eye be seen to form a basin, the rim of which lies over 300ft above sea level and with a radius of some three-quarters of a mile. **(1a)** At the centre of the basin there rises a tongue of high land, a narrow plateau at some 160-190ft in height. The prominence of this feature is both pin-pointed and accentuated today by the cathedral, which sits astride the plateau, known locally as the peninsula.

The rolling topography around Durham is of very recent geological origin. What we see today consists largely of thick drift deposits of sand, gravel and clay left by the Devensian ice-sheet (110,000 to 10,000 years ago) and subsequent melt-water lake overlying the original solid geology of the Lower Coal Measure Series. The drift not only contributes significantly to the prominent rim of the basin, but on the west side of the city is responsible for diverting southwards the course of the river Browney away from its original confluence with the Wear at Durham. **(1b, c)**

Following the disappearance of the ice and the reactivation of river systems on the new surface, the Wear had the major task of re-establishing its former alignment northwards. The alluvium deposits of its present flood plain show that it has meandered widely across the drift deposits in its effort to define a channel within its earlier valley. In the vicinity of Durham it has cut broad gaps, both to the south and north, through what was referred to above as the rim of the Durham basin. A wide or open valley floor is the result. Within the basin, however, the meandering river was thwarted where it encountered formerly buried solid rock. It was thus 'caught' and no longer able to migrate

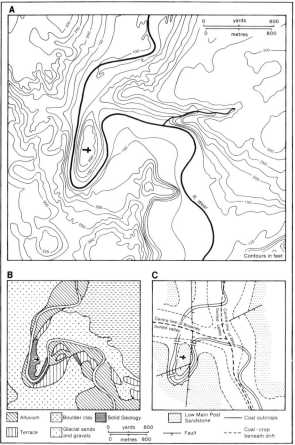

1 Durham's physical background: (a) relief, (b) solid geology, (c) drift geology.

Alluvium
Terrace
Boulder clay
Glacial sands and gravels
Solid Geology

Low Main Post Sandstone
Fault
Coal outcrops
Coal - crop beneath drift

Centre line of Browney buried valley
Centre line of Wear buried valley

R. Wear

Contours in feet

2 Aerial view of Durham from the south.

laterally. Energised by gentle isostatic uplift of the land no longer depressed by the weight of ice – approaching 1,000ft thick at its maximum, 18,000 years ago – the river cut down vertically in its established meander through the series of sandstone, shales and thin bands of coal. The result today is a horse-shoe loop in the middle of the Durham basin as the river curiously doubles back on itself in a gorge some 100ft deep. This 'incised meander' is the classic example of this physical feature cited in school and university textbooks. (The original research was undertaken by Arthur Holmes, Professor of Geology at the university.)[1]

The meander loop and the peninsula left upstanding as a result of the river's incision are unmistakable from a contour map. They are hardly less prominent in a modern aerial view, where their distinctiveness complements that of the instantly recognisable townscape silhouette at ground level. **(2)** It is as if nature has provided the city with an official seal or imprint. Meanwhile, it is entirely appropriate that the upstanding physical feature should have given its name to the city, Durham being Old English for 'hill-island'.

Prehistory

From some 10,000 years ago the extensive melt-waters occupying the Durham basin gradually gave way to damp lowlands with defined but winding water-courses that regularly inundated their flood plains. While reed beds occupied the shallow valleys, continued amelioration of the climate encouraged affor-estation of the higher and drier ground. The earliest human arrivals were hunter-gatherers of the Palaeolithic and Mesolithic eras, with the first few settler-farmers following in the Neolithic period from 3,000BC. The earliest prehistoric finds, mainly flint artefacts, are located on the southern rim of the basin, all above 300ft – at Elvet Hill, Little High Wood and Mountjoy Hill – with a single stray find nearby at Old Durham.[2] **(3)** Any conclusions derived from the distribution, however, must be tempered by the fact that our present knowledge is reliant on recorded evidence of excavations at recent construction sites or from stray finds.

More substantial evidence is in the form of the Iron Age hill-fort of Maiden Castle on the east rim of the basin. Its high, defensive site was even more pro-nounced when first constructed, when three of its four steep sides were lapped by meanders of the Wear.

Roman activity

Several separate finds on the peninsula indicate that from the first century AD the central plateau was for the first time a focus of activity. **(4)** Tantalisingly, however, no direct archaeological evidence of settlement has yet come to light, the findings being mainly pottery shards, a quern and coins. The settlement of which we do have knowledge is at what is known as Old Durham. Here, an original native farming unit had developed by the fourth century into a modest villa, judged by the evidence of a bath-house with accompanying *opus signinum* floors and a hypocaust.[3] Unfortunately all traces, including its circular thresh-ing floors, were destroyed by mineral extraction in the 1940s when the sand and gravel, which had originally provided a dry-point site in the wet lowland, was taken for the construction industry. **(5)**

Evidence of Roman roads in the city is hardly more convincing. The main military road, Dere Street, ran north through the county from Pierce Bridge on the Tees to the Wall at Corbridge. At present-day Willington, some 6 miles to the south-west of Durham, a branch can be traced aiming directly for the heart of the city, but evidence is lost beyond Stonebridge, 1½ miles short, on the ascent of the western rim. It has been suggested that at the top of the ridge the road then went north to Chester-le-Street – and thus on to Newcastle and

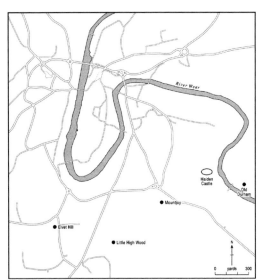

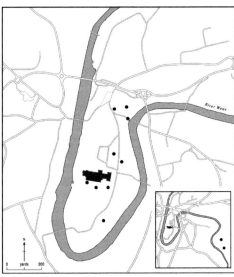

3 Prehistoric finds. In the background is the present road pattern.

4 Roman finds. In the background is the present road pattern.

5 The underground heating system of the Roman bathhouse, Old Durham, c.1940.

South Shields[4] – but it seems reasonable to infer that a link also descended the rim towards the peninsula.

A second, later road through the county, known as Cade's Road, is considered to have run from Middleton on the Tees, through Sedgefield to Chester-le-Street. Old Durham appears directly in line with its northerly course, and it is tempting to link it with wooden piers of a bridge in the river nearby, reportedly found in the early nineteenth century but since lost.

Early Saxon history

For most of the Saxon period it appears that the Durham area, possessing no immediate advantage in terms of accessibility, waterway or fertile soil, remained sparsely populated. The important settlements remained those established by the Romans at Chester-le-Street, 6 miles to the north, and Lanchester, 7 miles to the west. It may be noted that when religious houses were established in the seventh century during the golden age of Northumbria they were at Monkwearmouth (Sunderland) and Jarrow. Again, a century later, when the Lindisfarne Community fled south, they re-established themselves at Chester-le-Street.

The only occurrence that most commentators associate with early Durham is the consecration of Peohtwine as Bishop of Whithorn (Galloway) in 763 at *Aelflet ee* or Aelfet Island, translated as Elvet, the area immediately east of the peninsula in the vicinity of the present church dedicated to St Oswald (a Northumbrian king killed in battle in 642). The source is the *Anglo-Saxon*

Chronicle, and although the earliest maps of Durham *c*.1600 depict a circular churchyard, suggesting an ancient foundation, any supporting archaeological evidence of an early church building has proved elusive. (The church, anyway, would have been of wooden construction.) Moreover, archaeological finds in Elvet of any kind for the tenth to twelfth centuries are notable for their absence. Concentration was decidedly on the peninsula. **(6)**

There can be no doubt, however, about either the veracity or significance of an event in 995, in which Durham was chosen as the final resting place and shrine

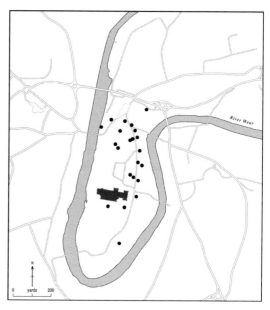

6 Tenth- to twelfth-century finds. In the background is the present road pattern.

for the North's most honoured saint. The presence of the enshrined body of St Cuthbert was to define the genius of the place, the character of the settlement, while the accompanying Community of St Cuthbert conferred on the city the privileges and regional influence through its extensive landed estates. It was the founding moment of the city, with roots that go back to the seventh century and the island of Lindisfarne or Holy Island.

St Cuthbert

Cuthbert was called to monastic life by a vision of the death of St Aidan, who had been brought by King Oswald from Iona in 635 to found a missionary house on Lindisfarne as a base for spreading the Christian faith in northern England. Following service at the sister houses of Melrose and Ripon, he became prior at the mother-house at Lindisfarne, eventually and reluctantly becoming Bishop of Lindisfarne in obedience to King Ecgfrith and Archbishop Theodore. His holiness, wisdom and learning, together with his association with miracle-working, attracted people to one who was essentially a contemplative at heart. And it was in chosen solitude that he died, in his cell on Inner

Farne in 687, having earlier resigned as bishop through failing health. He was buried, however, not on Inner Farne but beside the altar of the priory church.

In 698 Cuthbert was proclaimed a saint, affirmation of canonisation being given by the undecayed nature of his body when it was disinterred for translation to an elevated stone shrine. Bishop Eadfrith commissioned the sumptuously illustrated *Lindisfarne Gospels* for the shrine; it is today acknowledged as the earliest great masterpiece of English medieval book painting. At the same time a written record or testimony of the saint's life was commissioned and produced by an anonymous Lindisfarne brother. Bede followed soon after with both a verse and prose life of Cuthbert, besides giving fuller treatment in his *Ecclesiastical History of the English People* in 831.[5] Wonder-working relics beside the shrine added a further important dimension to the emerging legend and the 'cult' of St Cuthbert.

St Cuthbert Community

Within a century of Cuthbert's death the priory church had been rededicated and the community itself named after him (and not the founding saint, Aidan). Cuthbert, in fact, is the clearest example in all Anglo-Saxon England of a saint's culture binding together and guaranteeing continuity of a community during a period of political upheaval.[6] He was patron, as well as saint, seen as the guarantor through his continuing role as recipient and defender of the Community's lands and privileges.[7] When the community was forced to leave Lindisfarne in 875 under threat of Viking attack, they naturally took the body with them, along with the treasures and relics.

The community relocated several times during a period of political upheaval in Northumbria, but during this time it not only preserved but extended its estates and had rights confirmed. **(7a)** Although possession of the body of their dead, yet still active, leader is recorded as of crucial importance, location of their estates and a series of shrewd political alliances together offer an explanation of the community's history before eventual arrival at Durham.

After various halts on Community holdings during the seven years of wanderings across northern England there was a more permanent stop at Chester-le-Street from 882. Choice of this location was not unrelated to the gift to the Community by Danish king Guthred of much of the territory between the rivers Tyne and Tees. (Earlier, Abbot Eadred had been instructed in a vision to advise the Danes to elect Guthred as their king.) The new location was certainly more optimally located with regard to the Community's new territories, compared with the peripheral position of Lindisfarne. **(7b)**

The body was enshrined at Chester-le-Street in a wooden cathedral dedicated to St Mary and St Cuthbert, within the confines of the old Roman town, until in 995 renewed Viking threat caused another upheaval. The community fled south to Ripon, but after a few months they started on the return journey, presumably intending to re-establish their base at Chester-le-Street. They never got that far, stopping 6 miles short at Durham, which became their final resting place.

A political explanation for the decision seems likely, for the leader of the community at this time, Bishop Aldun, had powerful family connections in the area. His son-in-law, Uchtred, was the rising Earl of Northumbria of the House of Bamburgh. (He subsequently played a key role in the building of a new church, and erected defences around the crest of the peninsula.) Aldun can hardly have been ignorant of the potential of Durham, having been bishop for some forty years while residing a mere 7 miles away. Durham was no less optimally located than Chester-le-Street with regard to the community's lands, besides offering a far superior defensible site. Security was heightened by the river, which lapped around the near-vertical sides of the gorge, while at the same time its lack of navigability offered no hope to any would-be invading Viking longboat.

Interpretation of the decision to locate at Durham may be supplemented or enriched by a mythic or legendary history in which the events are certified in word and picture. Thus Symeon, a Benedictine monk at Durham writing in the early twelfth century, records how the cart bearing Cuthbert's coffin became immoveable – 'firmly fixed as it were a mountain' – on the return journey at Wardlaw, and was only released after three days of fasting, prayer and vigil, during which it was revealed to one of their number that the saint wished his home to be at 'Dunholme'.[8]

The *Rites of Durham* of 1594 embellishes the story further in recording that, according to oral tradition, the exact whereabouts of Dunholme was learnt from overhearing a milkmaid referring to a stray cow at the location.[9] A bas-relief sculpture related to this story is on the north-west corner of the transept of the Chapel of Nine Altars.

Sir Walter Scott further certified the story in his long poem 'Marmion'. Canto 2 recounts the early history, not least the ecclesiastical history, of Northumbria,

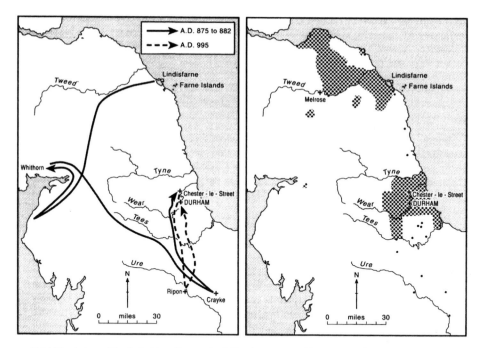

7 (a) Wanderings of the St Cuthbert Community. (b) Lands, estates and houses sometime attached to the St Cuthbert Community.

in which Cuthbert and his wanderings are outlined. The latter episode concludes with:

> Chester-le-Street, and Ripon, saw
> His holy corpse, ere Wardilaw
> Hailed him with joy and fear;
> And, after many wanderings passed,
> He chose his lordly seat at last,
> Where his cathedral, huge and vast,
> Looks down upon the Wear.[10]

In recent times a further, and unlikely, source to depict Durham's holy beginnings is the railway poster by Doris Zinkeisen, c.1930. **(8)** Unlikely the source may be, but no other illustration better encapsulates the story of our city. Based on medieval manuscripts but executed in art nouveau and art deco style, it portrays the translation of St Cuthbert's body, with clear reference to the foundation of the earlier cathedral as well as its contemporary silhouette. The motley group is led by a piper, and Bishop Aldun is followed by monks and

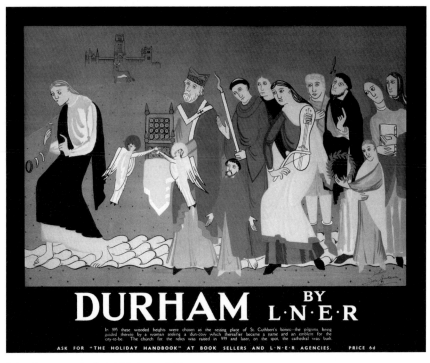

8 A railway poster by Doris Zinkeisen, c.1930.

others. The *Lindisfarne Gospels* is suggested by the book that one is carrying. The coffin is watched over by two angels, while, distant and above all, their destination is suggested by a cow on top of a rounded mound, and the saint's ultimate resting place by a faint outline of the Norman cathedral.

The year 995, then, was the founding moment of our city. Once at their destination the Community immediately erected a cover for the coffin of branches or wattle and daub, which was soon replaced by a stone structure, known as the 'White Church', presumably on account of the lighter hue of the freshly cut sandstone. One author has recently suggested that this building might have been the church of St Oswald, just off the peninsula.[11] The stone structure itself was only temporary, for in 998 another structure ('Ecclesia Major') was begun, with Uchtred impressing the whole population between the rivers Tees and Coquet for the task of raising a cathedral worthy to contain the shrine of their saint. It was completed in 1017, a substantial building with towers over the choir and west end.

The mantle of the country's leading pilgrimage centre thus fell on Durham. Its attraction was soon further boosted in the first half of the eleventh century

Northumbria is noted for a 'golden age' during the second half of the seventh and eighth centuries, when the Anglo-Saxon kingdom was the source of a remarkable flowering of English art and culture. Its beginning is traceable to 635 when King Oswald invited Aidan and some Irish monks from Iona to re-introduce Christianity to North East England from a base on the island at Lindisfarne. Gradually a series of monasteries covered the region, the most important houses being at Hexham, Ripon, Whitby and, especially, the joint foundation of Monkwearmouth-Jarrow.

The coming together of Anglo-Saxon, Irish, or Celtic, and Mediterranean influence was the stimulus for the sumptuously illustrated manuscripts, also for embroidery, carved artefacts in bone and metal, as well as heavily incised stone crosses. Lindisfarne and Monkwearmouth-Jarrow in particular were intellectual powerhouses. In the latter monastery Bede, the most famous scribe, wrote over forty works on history, sermons, poems and science, many of which were circulated throughout Europe. (He benefited from the vast library built up at Jarrow through several visits to the continent by the monastery's founder, Benedict Biscop.) At Whitby, Caedmon is acknowledged to be one of the earliest, if not the earliest, writer of Anglo-Saxon poetry.

Circulation of manuscripts apart, the influence of Northumbria spread far beyond its borders. Missionaries were sent to Scotland at the request of the Picts; missionaries also founded the church in Mercia. Northumbrians abroad included Wilfred and Willibrord as missionaries in Frisia, the latter being made bishop; Willebrad, who became bishop of Bremen; and Alcuin, adviser to Charlemagne in Aachen and abbot of Tours.

The golden age foundered towards the end of the eighth century, weakened by internal political instability and Viking attack from without. Today its legacy is preserved in Durham, the community of Cuthbert having brought both the saint's body and treasures to the city, to which later were added the remains of Bede, and other manuscripts. It is a legacy that is annually commemorated in a cathedral service giving thanks to its 'founders and benefactors'; and it is a legacy acknowledged in the naming of five of the colleges of the university.

by the acquisition of more relics and bones of several other holy men, the most notable being those of St Boisil, prior at Melrose when Cuthbert first entered monastic life, and, especially, of the Venerable Bede from Jarrow monastery. The acquisitions were the 'work' of an active sacrist of Durham, Elfred Westhou, who was clearly a most energetic exponent of this particular medieval practice.

Further wealth and gifts were brought by pilgrims, whose needs must have stimulated the provision of infrastructure to support them. And from such beginnings, of course, there was to emerge the present-day tourist activity. Among the early visitors was King Cnut (Canute), who is recorded as walking 5 miles barefoot from Trimdon in 1031. On his visit the King of England gifted further lands and confirmed the privileges of the community. The latter act suggests that the relationship between king and community was to their mutual benefit. From the point of view of the community, it may be seen as conforming to previous shrewd alliances that had been forged with Northumbrian and Danish royal households. The question they were soon about to face was what type of relationship would there be with a royal house from Normandy.

two

ANGLO-NORMAN DURHAM

Norman Arrival

The decades both preceding and following the Norman Conquest can appropriately be described as volatile. Before the Conquest there remained the possibility of Scottish incursion into the area, with the city itself besieged in 1039 (by Duncan, later to be murdered by Macbeth) and 1061. On neither occasion were the peninsula defences breached. From mid-century, annoyance as much as danger emanated from two successive Earls of Northumbria. The rule of both ended prematurely, but not before each in turn had appointed bishops to the see of Durham without consulting the Community of Cuthbert.

In view of the complexity of the northernmost province of his new kingdom, it is little wonder that William the Conqueror should experience difficulty and setbacks before achieving a degree of stability. His initial strategy was to govern through native deputies, allowing Northumbrian nobles to retain the earldom. They proved unsuitable appointments. The first, Copsig, was assassinated within a matter of weeks in 1067; his successor, Cospatric, was of dubious loyalty and lasted little longer, having to flee to Scotland in 1068. William therefore turned to one of his own barons, Robert Cumin, and sent him north with a contingent of 700 soldiers. In 1069 he billeted the company within the city for the night, but before dawn a Northumbrian force, probably with local connivance, burst through the gates, killed the unsuspecting troops and setting fire to the bishop's palace where Cumin was lodged. 'So great, at the last, was the multitude of the slain,' recorded Symeon, 'that every street was covered with blood, and filled with dead bodies'.[11] A single wounded soldier is reported to have survived.

St Cuthbert is mentioned in the massacre story in that he is reputed to have changed the wind direction from north to east, thus blowing the flames from the palace away from the church. There is no mention of the bishop himself.

Perhaps he acted on the news of a plot, which he is said to have imparted to Cumin at a meeting beforehand, and absented himself.

The Conqueror's response was devastating, even if the first garrison he dispatched turned back at Allerton because of a mist attributed to St Cuthbert. During the winter of 1069–70, however, the king's forces undertook a 'harrying of the north', laying waste every village between York and Durham as punishment and in order to prevent any subsequent insurrection.

William himself reached Durham in early 1070. The community, however, had fled. Having been alerted to the impending visit, Bishop Aethewin considered it prudent to lead them back to Lindisfarne, taking St Cuthbert's coffin and treasures. Their sojourn was brief, however, as they returned after three months, having first sent one of their number to gauge safety. After some repair, cleaning and re-consecration of the cathedral, their former life was resumed. Bishop Aethewin, however, was soon to flee the country, having heard of William's treatment of Anglo-Saxon clergy, from which even the Archbishop of Canterbury was not exempt.

Although the Conqueror had found no clerical presence on his visit, the size of both church and diocese, together with knowledge of the regional significance of the Cuthbert connection, will have confirmed Durham's importance for his political strategy. Moreover, the defensive qualities of the peninsula were self-evident: it was the first suitable site north of the Tees, and with a convenient situation in this unpacified part of his kingdom.

Bishop Walcher

Accordingly, in 1071 William appointed Walcher from Lorraine as bishop, the first in a line of non-hereditary bishops. On a visit the following year the king commissioned the building of a castle, which was to be both fortress and a new episcopal palace. (Waltham Abbey was to provide the revenue for its construction.) There was to be no repetition of the massacre of Robert Cumin and his men. An earth motte or mound was built up, mostly material from a ditch around its southern edge. A timber tower was erected on top; otherwise building in the bailey or inner courtyard was in stone. **(9a)** The earliest remaining part is the Norman crypt chapel, usually given the date of 1072 but probably originating a few years later. Certainly today it constitutes a stunning, intimate architectural space, with two rows of three columns with marked sandstone

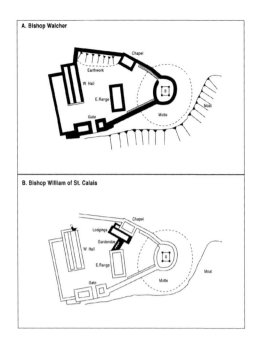

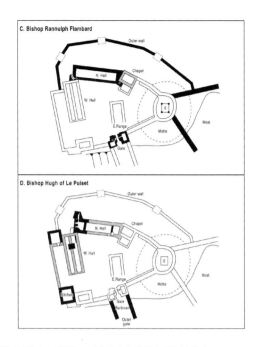

9 The evolution of Durham Castle: (a) Bishop Walcher (1071–80), (b) Bishop William of St Calais (1081–96), (c) Bishop Rannulph Flambard (1099-1128), (d) Bishop Hugh of Le Puiset (1153–95).

veining and sculptured capitals. Much original herringbone paving remains. (10) Little light enters through a small window set in the extremely thick north wall, which formed part of the defences.

While the Conqueror was in the city, Symeon records how the king asked to see the allegedly uncorrupt body of St Cuthbert, threatening the life of senior churchmen if pilgrims had been deceived. Immediately before the crucial moment the king 'was suddenly seized with an excessive heat', such that he immediately mounted his horse and did not stop until he had crossed the Tees.[2] Intervention of St Cuthbert apart, it is possible that the monks themselves took the initiative in order to achieve what they had obtained from previous monarchs, namely confirmation of their rights and privileges.

In 1075 Bishop Walcher acquired further powers when the king sold him the earldom of Northumbria, following the execution of Waltheof for implication in a plot against the monarchy. In taking over the civil duties of the earldom, the bishop became both secular and ecclesiastical head of the region. Such were his civil, judicial and military powers that he was in effect a prince-bishop: viceroy to the king in a region far from the capital. The County Palatinate was brought into being, and the coat of arms of the bishops of Durham henceforward reflected their special status, being set against a sword and crosier, not two crosiers, and by a mitre above the coat of arms being encircled with a coronet.

The out-working of the first County Palatine was uneasy, and ultimately proved disastrous, less because of the novelty of a spiritual head acting in civil government, but more in the people to whom delegated powers were given. Relations with Northumbrians had reached a low ebb when Bishop Walcher went to meet them in council at Gateshead, and was assassinated. The king's immediate response was to send his brother Odo, Bishop of Bayeux, and his troops to exact revenge through a second round of laying waste.

Before his death Bishop Walcher had taken the first steps towards a reordering of monasticism at Durham. He was confirmed in his desire with the arrival, in 1074, of

10 Norman chapel, Durham Castle.

Aldwin, Prior of Winchcombe in Gloucestershire, who had felt the call to introduce disciplined Benedictine communities into the ravaged wastelands of the North East. Aldwin and his two companions made initially for Newcastle, but Walcher offered them a base at St Paul's, Jarrow. Although a ruin, its association with Bede could hardly fail to attract them. Their success persuaded the bishop to grant the new community estuarine lands along the Tyne. Soon afterwards, in 1078, the bishop began building a dormitory at Durham adjacent to the cathedral, the first part of a future Benedictine monastery. Had he survived, it was his intention to become one of their order. His broader vision, however, was to be realised, and realised in spectacular fashion, by his successors. Three remarkable bishops from Normandy were to imprint on the city its present Norman outline and appearance.

Bishop William of St Calais

William of St Calais was abbot of St Vincent in Normandy and had already come to the notice of the King of France and the Pope before the Conqueror appointed him to the see of Durham in 1081. His abilities were wide-ranging – from the spiritual and intellectual to business and political. He was a key adviser to the Conqueror and favourite minister to his successor, William

Rufus. Among his influence at court was the key role he played in planning and organising the Domesday Survey. When a three-year exile is taken into account, it seems that he was in fact absent longer than he was present in the diocese, such that one author has concluded that 'his place was at the heart of the administration of the realm rather than in the episcopal chair of the church of St Cuthbert'.[3] Be that as it may, the achievements of St William of Calais at Durham were crucially significant.

In turning his attention to the existing community of St Cuthbert, as a monk he must have considered it irregular to find no communal living or rule of celibacy at Durham. The existing community consisted of a dean, seven senior priests, who were descendants of those who were the original coffin-bearers, and an unspecified number of junior priests and clerks, together with their families. It must have appeared incongruous to have such a community serving the mother church of the diocese, while nearby at Jarrow and at Monkwearmouth there were recently established Benedictine communities. A further point of which Bishop William will have been aware was that the members of the present community had loyalties reaching deep into the Anglo-Saxon past.[4]

Before moving to reorganise the community, the bishop secured the permission of the king (and queen), Archbishop of Canterbury and the Pope – the last obtained while in Rome on the king's business. To legitimacy he added continuity, stressing that it was a return to a regular life of observance of the founders, as recorded by Bede. In this respect Symeon's writings may be interpreted as an important contribution to the justification of continuity and inheritance to the Lindisfarne legacy – and to the claims of the new Priory at Durham to church lands in north Northumbria.[5]

In 1083, therefore, twenty-three monks were brought from Jarrow and Monkwearmouth, with Aldwin the first prior. Members of the existing community were given the opportunity of becoming monks. Only one – the dean – accepted; the remainder were settled in collegiate churches in the south of the diocese.

In 1087 Aldwin died after fourteen years of significant influence on monastic life in the North East. He was succeeded by his disciple and companion Turgot. Fortunately his successor was adroit at administration, for he was called upon during Bishop William's absences at court – and during the bishop's three-year exile, 1088–91, when he found himself looking after the diocese in addition to governing the monastery.

William of St Calais maintained his high profile with King William Rufus, who succeeded to the throne in 1087. Soon, however, he was implicated in a threat to have Rufus replaced by the Conqueror's eldest son, whom his father had made Duke of Normandy. (The rebellion was led by the Conqueror's half-brother, Odo, Bishop of Bayeux. Bayeux is where William of St Calais began his career.) Despite being accused of treason, he eventually emerged victorious, even negotiating an allowance for his maintenance in exile and persuading the Pope to remonstrate against Rufus over his ill treatment. Bishop William was therefore restored to office, with the improbable outcome in September 1091 of arriving back in Durham and being escorted into his castle by both the King of England and the Duke of Normandy. The two brothers had been reconciled, primarily by the threat of a Scottish invasion.

11 An eleventh-century manuscript with a depiction of Bishop William of St Calais.

The castle was extensively developed during Bishop William's episcopacy so that the inner bailey was surrounded by ranges to the north, west and east, while to the south the gatehouse was remodelled. **(9b)** William of St Calais, however, left a more lasting legacy at the southern end of Palace Green.

From his exile he brought back gifts for the new abbey, not least a large and valuable collection of books and manuscripts. They represent a high point in manuscript writing and decoration. Nearly half of some fifty volumes have survived to contribute to the largest number of volumes *in situ* of any monastic house in the country. Intriguingly, in one eleventh-century commentary on the psalms there appears a full-length depiction of Bishop William. **(11)** By now a south range of monastic buildings had been added to Bishop Walcher's east range, and the current incumbent considered it opportune to turn his attention to a major, accompanying project.

Bishop William had brought back with him more than gifts for the new abbey, namely the conviction that Aldun's cathedral, although less than 100 years old, was not the appropriate structure to express the new ecclesiastical and secular reality. The Normans had already replaced Anglo-Saxon cathedrals with their own buildings in various parts of England, and Durham was to benefit from its lateness in this sequence, also from its important strategic location far from London. Above all there was the genius of William of St Calais, who, besides bringing back resources to begin constructing a new church, had clearly been observant while in the heartland of Romanesque building in Normandy during his time abroad.

As patron, quite apart from being paymaster, it is reasonable to assume that, although not the architect, he was responsible for the design brief that incorporated his accumulated knowledge and vision to emulate the best in Europe. If massing and design derived from his experience in Normandy, then scale and some elements of detailing can be attributed to his visit to Rome. Thus, symbolically, the overall length, width and three-apsed end of the building was to be the same as St Peter's itself, with a further association in its spiral columns at its east end, where there was to be the shrine of the saint. **(12)** In architectural terms the high stone rib-vaulting in the choir was to be the earliest in Europe, while the elaborate decoration surpassed any of its contemporaries.[6] **(13)**

As a replacement for the existing cathedral – a not inconsiderable structure in itself – the scale change might be gauged from a comparison of the ground plans of the two buildings. **(14)** If the reconstruction of the Saxon cloister and church by Hope,[7] based on archaeological investigation and conjecture, is anywhere near accurate , then Bishop William's design would seem to be more than twice the length and four times the width. And, of course, it soared to a much greater height.

In July 1093, having ordered the destruction of the Saxon church, the bishop and Prior Turgot dug the first foundation; in August the foundation stones were laid in the presence of the bishop, prior and King Malcolm of Scotland. The last-named was on his way to Gloucester for peace talks with William Rufus. It is interesting to note that soon afterwards the building of

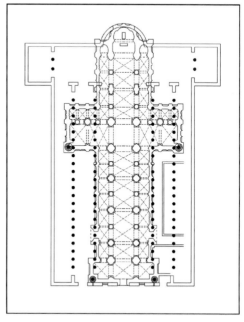

12 The plan of Durham Cathedral of 1133 superimposed on a plan of Old St Peter's, Rome.

13 Durham Cathedral: the nave looking east.

14 A comparison of ground plans of the Norman cathedral with the conjectured Saxon cathedral.

Lindisfarne Priory, now daughter-house of Durham, was begun, presumably as acknowledgement of its origin. (Apart from scale and use of red sandstone, the design brief appeared almost identical to that of the new mother-house – three-storey elevation, alternation of compound and cylindrical piers, rib-vaulting, incised decoration and chevrons.) **(15)**

William of St Calais died just three years into the building programme, by which time only the lower courses of the east end can have been completed, but the monks continued building the church until 1099, when Ranulf Flambard was appointed bishop. Before continuing the narrative, however, one further action of Bishop William should be recorded.

When William of St Calais returned from exile in Normandy in 1091 he brought with him not only the blueprint for the new cathedral and gifts for the monastery but also the scribe Symeon. Known as 'Symeon of Durham', the writings of this monk are the major source of information of the monastery of Durham and its community from the time of Bede. As chief scribe he was given the task by his elders of writing the history of the priory and community. In so-doing, as mentioned above, he not unnaturally legitimises the whole enterprise: neither Viking raiding and certainly not Norman succession (with a celibate

Benedictine order installed to replace the community of clerks) interrupted the continuity from Oswald and Aidan to Bede and beyond. The body of Cuthbert, together with its associated treasures, not least the *Lindisfarne Gospels*, was a tangible part of the legitimation. In short, the church in Durham was the church of Lindisfarne recreated – and, by implication, the legitimate inheritor of its lands and churches.

Bishop Rannulph Flambard

Flambard was a controversial and colourful figure, who survived an assassination attempt, imprisonment in the Tower of London (from which he escaped) and pardon from Henry II for persuading Robert, Duke of Normandy to join forces on an invasion to overthrow the monarch.

15 Lindisfarne Priory.

A recent author has branded him as a kind of James Bond of the medieval episcopate who 'laid no claim to spirituality and took little heed of morality'.[8] He served as minister and treasurer to William Rufus and was a manipulator of money, including the selling of bishoprics. On his deathbed he made a full confession of his sins to the monks and people of Durham, but certainly during the twenty-nine years he was bishop he contributed massively to the consolidation of the city.[9]

Construction of the cathedral continued apace. Within five years the east end was ready for St Cuthbert's coffin to be translated from the remaining part of the old cathedral into the new. Days before, Prior Turgot and several monks had opened the coffin and found the robed body of St Cuthbert to be uncorrupt. The bones of Bede and head of St Oswald were in an inner coffin with various treasures, not least *St Cuthbert's Gospel*, a leather-bound copy of St John's Gospel now acknowledged to be the oldest intact European book. An undecayed body naturally drew scepticism – not least among Norman overlords, who had only recently succeeded to the inheritance surrounding

16 'The building of Durham'. A detail of a mural by Thomas Pattison, County Hall, Durham, 1963.

the most famous Anglo-Saxon saint – and therefore a further examination was undertaken in the presence of independent witnesses, including the Abbot of Seez. The body was lifted up and arms and legs were moved to show flexibility. All were convinced, and on 4 September 1104 the coffin was borne in procession to a new shrine behind the high altar.[10]

The westward construction of the church continued through Flambard's long period in office, and was virtually completed by the end of his episcopate. One index of the scale of the operation can be seen in the recognisable signatures or marks of 179 stonemasons. Other marks, stone infillings some 6in square, indicate where builders' scaffolding was inserted in the walls during the construction. An imaginative depiction of the building operation in progress can be seen in a large mural in County Hall. **(16)** From about 1110 the distinctive zig-zag or chevron decoration motif in ribs and vaulting made its appearance, the first in northern Europe. By his death in 1128 the building was complete apart from some nave vaulting and the west towers. The latter may well have had a dual role in that they were to be incorporated into the western perimeter defences. Indeed, the generous upper galleries of the massive structure in general may have been designed to offer a potential military role.[11] In more than external appearance, then, Sir Walter Scott's description of the cathedral as 'Half church of God, half castle 'gainst the Scot' is not inappropriate.

The castle also underwent major reconstruction during Bishop Flambard's time.[12] **(9c)** A prestigious new great hall at the northern end of the courtyard reflected its role as an episcopal palace, while the gatehouse was relocated to provide a visually impressive processional way to the cathedral. Other additions emphasised and strengthened its role as a fortress. A new outer defensive wall with towers formed a semicircle around the north of the site. A wall was extended both to the east to a mighty North Gate, guarding the only entry from the neck of the peninsula, and also to the east end of the cathedral. Palace

Green thus became an enclosed, walled space between castle and cathedral, a space full of dwellings that Flambard proceeded to clear, ostensibly on grounds of fire risk and pollution, although the betterment of context of both palace and cathedral was probably a stronger motive.

The building of walls, castle and, not least, cathedral and monastery took a vast amount of stone, much beyond that which could be supplied by quarries around the peninsula riverbanks. The Low Main Post (Cathedral) sandstone, some 35ft in thickness and capable of being masoned into blocks for building, formed the lip of the gorge and was exposed in the gorge sides. It was readily worked during earlier constructions, perhaps too readily in some places. The vast buttresses later required to make safe the Galilee chapel may be an example of over-zealous extraction, while a little further to the north the section known as Broken Walls may derive from similar activity. On the banks the most extensive evidence today of working is the Sacrist's Quarry, a wide dell on the outside of the south-west bend in the river, and the Great Quarry, an elongated working immediately below the line of South Street.

The more extensive quantities of stone required were still relatively close at hand, for it has been calculated by geologists that the volume of stone removed from a large quarry immediately west of South Street would have been sufficient for both cathedral and monastic buildings.[13] Other quarries, presumed to be of slightly later date, were in the next gorge section 2 miles downriver at Kepier and in Baxter Wood on the Browney, a mile to the west.

Also in stone, and one of the earliest stone bridges in England since the Roman era, was Framwellgate Bridge, built by Flambard in the shadow of the castle in 1128. It connected the Bishop's Borough, with its market on the neck of the peninsula, with the Prior's Borough of Crossgate to the west. Bridging two landfalls of similar height was a less demanding task here than that on the eastern side of the peninsula, but the key feature may well have been that the region's main north-south route skirted the river on the western side of the peninsula. A further point is that construction of a weir to power the Bishop's Mill, just downstream, would have deepened the water, thereby making fording the river no longer possible. Half a mile downriver the bishop founded Kepier Hospital (1112) as a hostel for pilgrims, with the associated church of St Giles on the crest above, around which the village of St Giles evolved. It stood on the route to Sherburn Hospital and Monkwearmouth.

Bishops Geoffrey Rufus and William of St Barbara

Bishop Flambard was followed by two successors of contrasting fortunes before the Norman era drew to a close with a third colourful and distinguished bishop.

After Flambard's death there was a five-year interregnum, during which time the monks continued constructing the cathedral, so that Bishop William Rufus (1133–40) found the building almost completed when he arrived. It had been erected in exactly forty years. Bishop Rufus was responsible for two doors in the south aisle of the nave linking to the abbey cloisters, the Prior's Door to the east and Monks' Door to the west. The latter retains its original strap-iron tracery. The chapter house was also constructed at this time. In addition Rufus was the first bishop to mint his own coins.

In the world beyond Durham at this time there was turmoil and civil strife, as King Stephen, the Conqueror's grandson, tried to ward off the legitimate claims of Matilda, only surviving child of Henry I. Matilda's uncle was David I of Scotland, who twice impinged on the history of Durham. In 1138 he had invaded England, and although defeated at the Battle of the Standard (near Northallerton), was bought off from future forays with the grant of the earldom of Northumberland in the Treaty of Durham. It was restored in 1157 under Henry II.

The second occasion occurred on the death of Bishop Rufus and coincided with Matilda's brief ascendancy to the English throne, when he encouraged William Cumin to succeed to the vacant see. Cumin, who was chancellor to King David and had been chaplain to Bishop Rufus, needed little encouragement. He occupied the castle, attempted to prevent monks escaping south to report on the situation, and even forged letters from the Pope endorsing his election. Eventually William of St Barbara was elected bishop, but it took more than a year to oust the usurper Cumin, and not before the latter had wreaked havoc in Elvet, Gilesgate and even the cathedral. Not surprisingly, Bishop William's episcopate (1143–52) was largely devoted to repairing the damage to fabric and persons.

Bishop Hugh of Le Puiset

Hugh of Le Puiset has been called the most princely of Durham's prince bishops. Certainly, lifestyle apart, the Palatinate reached its maximum extent during his episcopate when, in addition to buying the earldom of Northumberland, in 1189 he acquired the wapentake of Sadberge (crown-land immediately north of the Tees) from Richard I.

A cousin of Henry II, Hugh of Le Puiset travelled to Rome to be consecrated before his enthronement in Durham at the age of twenty-five. That he was below the canonical age for a bishop, or that he had already fathered three children by different mothers, was apparently no handicap. He later became Chief Judiciary and co-regent of all England, posts he held while the king was abroad. Le Puiset wished to join the monarch on the third crusade, and indeed prepared lavishly so to do, but the king, Richard I, the Lionheart, preferred to rely on his money-raising and administrative abilities at home. These abilities were put into practice, not least in levying funds to secure the king's release when he was imprisoned in southern Germany and held to ransom on his return journey from the Holy Land. The story of the discovery of his whereabouts by his minstrel, Blondel, is better known than Le Puiset's collection of ransom money.

In Durham Bishop Le Puiset left his mark in many projects. To the cathedral he added the Galilee chapel (1175) at its western extremity, after abortive attempts to extend at the east end, where the unconsolidated geology proved too challenging. The celibate Benedictine order ascribed the failure of the first efforts to the disapproval of St Cuthbert of having a lady chapel in the vicinity of his shrine. (A line of Frosterley marble was thus set in the floor at the back of the nave to mark the point beyond which women were confined.) Built in the remaining space between the west door of the cathedral and the very edge of the gorge, the chapel is wider than it is long. The main external entrance was through the north wall, while access to the nave was through the great west door, either side of which arched recesses were cut as sites for altars.

The chapel is notable for its slender, paired columns and round-headed, richly chevroned arches. **(17)** The former were of Purbeck marble from Dorset, the first non-local stone to be introduced into the cathedral, and obviously considered a fashionable addition. The lightness of this late or transitional Romanesque design suggests knowledge of French Gothic architecture; the quality of light encourages some to perceive a Moorish influence to this arcaded hall. It also retains sufficient of its original wall-painting to illustrate how colourful the space must have once appeared.

The bulk of the chapel was originally covered in non-decorative painting, as was the stonework throughout the cathedral,[14] but the surviving architectural

17 The Galilee chapel.

polychromy of the spandrels and arcade leading to the altar in the second bay from the north – Our Lady of Pity's altar – is especially noteworthy.[15] Here can be seen various depictions of crucifixion, St Paul being beheaded, Adam rising from the grave and, nearer the east wall, three monks of Durham in Benedictine habit. **(18)** On the two recesses of the altar are full length figures of a bishop and king, possibly St Cuthbert **(19)** and St Oswald. Pittington church, a mere 3 miles distant and built by the architect who designed the Galilee chapel, contains a wall painting attributed to the same artist, which shows Cuthbert being consecrated bishop by Archbishop Theodore. The extensive use of a rich blue pigment, ultramarine, the most expensive of all pigments in the Middle Ages and originating from mines in Afghanistan, is an indication of the wealth of the abbey.

The new chapel was graced by an impressive shrine on a pedestal with a canopy over for St Bede. His remains had formerly lain alongside St Cuthbert in the feretory.

With the new chapel to be in front of the great west door of the cathedral, Le Puiset had earlier constructed a new main entrance and porch to the cathedral, the great north door, complete with sanctuary knocker, in 1154. The

Above 18 A wall painting, north spandrel in the Galilee chapel.

Right 19 A wall painting of a bishop, possibly St Cuthbert, Our Lady of Pity's altar, Galilee chapel.

bronze head, cast in Durham, is beyond compare among Romanesque door rings.[16] **(20)** On the mainland of Europe the nearest similar mask is at Le Puy Cathedral in France. Although referred to as a knocker, it is in fact a fixed ring with no striking plate behind. After shouting to attract attention while clasping the handle held in the serrated teeth of the grotesque head, a fugitive was admitted by two men stationed in a small room above the door. Sanctuary consisted of confession and several days' sojourn wearing a special cloak, before choice of trial or safe passage to the nearest port and exile abroad. The right of sanctuary, first granted by Danish King Guthred and confirmed by King Alfred, clearly continued during the Norman era. St Cuthbert had prophesied in 687 that his body would become a goal for 'fugitives and guilty men of every sort' seeking sanctuary.

Under Le Puiset the monastery was 'at the height of its literary and intellectual distinction, magnificently housed in one of the most superb churches of western Christendom, and endowed with the enormous name of Cuthbert, and the wealth of a patrimony, containing the best part of the one-time kingdom of Northumbria'.[17] The bishop himself gave over seventy books to the monastery, a benefaction of similar importance to that of William of St Calais. Thirteen of these survive.[18]

At this time the monastery had no fewer than nine outlying daughter-houses and cells, stretching from Lindisfarne to Stamford and Oxford, where there was

a study house. At the mother-house more than fifty monks lived according to the Benedictine rule, while at the same time running an efficient business managing its estates, finances and everyday needs, quite apart from the numerous pilgrims visiting the country's most famous shrine. St Cuthbert was also well known on mainland Europe, not least as a result of the writings of Bede. In 1170, however, midway through the episcopacy of Le Puiset, the murder of Archbishop Becket at Canterbury threatened the popularity of the northern shrine. The response was immediate, and one of which modern image-makers would approve.

Durham's own qualities were reassessed and repackaged by Reginald, one of the monks. He

20 The sanctuary knocker on the cathedral's north door.

assiduously catalogued all the miracles attributed to Cuthbert, not least while the saint's body rested in Durham. Moreover, the miracles attributed to another local saint, Godric, who had recently died, were added to boost the attraction. Godric had been a hermit at Finchale, 3 miles downriver, and his beard was now added to the relics of the cathedral.

The castle also bears the indelible imprint of Bishop Le Puiset, not least in the extensive decorative sculptural stonework that was added as the building became decidedly an episcopal palace. Much repair was necessitated following a serious fire, which spread from the town and entirely gutted the west range and adjoining part of the north range. To the former he added a kitchen tower, while the north range was entirely rebuilt to comprise two halls, one above the other.

21 The ceremonial entrance to Bishop Le Puiset's great hall, Durham Castle.

To the lower one he built a magnificent ceremonial entrance with chevrons, rosettes and panelwork, now considered to be one of the finest examples of late Norman stone carving in this country. **(21)** As the principal entrance to the building, it was positioned to be in line with the gatehouse and reached up a flight of steps. Above, as part of the upper hall, the Norman gallery still retains particularly splendid arcading around its window bays. **(22)**

Immediately beyond the peninsula Le Puiset built the multi-arched Elvet Bridge (c.1170), the link to the Prior's Borough of Elvet, and gave instructions for the rebuilding of Elvet, which had been burnt down in Cumin's time, but refused the prior's request for a market. The Market Place, at the centre of the Bishop's Borough, was to have the monopoly of trade.[19] Thus in 1179 he granted the burgesses of his borough the city's first charter. Situated on the neck of the peninsula between the two bridges, and boosted by people uprooted from Palace Green, the area was the natural commercial focus. The burgesses were given important advantages over those who lived outside or who came to trade in Bishop's Borough. The charter made no mention of corporate self-government, for which the city had to wait nearly another four centuries.

22 Norman gallery, north hall, Durham Castle.

In the vicinity of the city the bishop rebuilt Kepier Hospital and St Giles's church, built a hospital at Witton Gilbert and another for lepers and their chaplains at Sherburn, while at Finchale a charter was granted for the founding of a priory. Wider afield Bishop Le Puiset is associated with organising a detailed survey of the bishopric, known as the Bolden Book after the village in which the survey started. The king's surveyors of the earlier Domesday Book had stopped short, south of the Tees.

The Anglo-Norman Settlement

By the end of the Norman period, which lasted little more than a century, the city had been given an indelible imprint. (23) A line of bishops – each talented, determined, resilient, if imperfect – succeeded to the early Anglo-Saxon beginnings and gave rise, both in core detail and outline, to the essential city as we know it today.

At the heart of the medieval city stood the cathedral, the great abbey church, dedicated to Christ, the Blessed Virgin Mary and St Cuthbert, monumental in scale, the climax of the High Romanesque, an engineering benchmark and a building by which others are now judged. Nearby was the imposing castle, fortress without and palace within. Together they dominated the peninsula, the

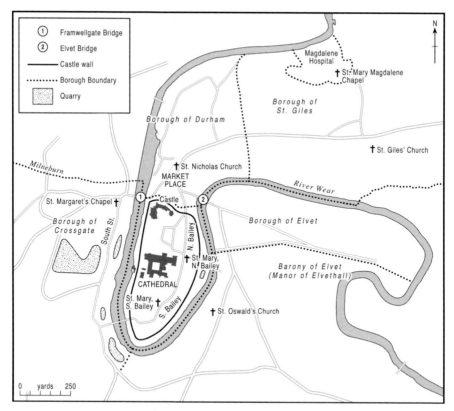

Key:
① Framwellgate Bridge
② Elvet Bridge
— Castle wall
········· Borough Boundary
▢ Quarry

Magdalene Hospital
✝ St. Mary Magdalene Chapel
Borough of St. Giles
✝ St. Giles' Church
Borough of Durham
Milneburn
✝ St. Nicholas Church
MARKET PLACE
St. Margaret's Chapel ✝
Castle
Borough of Crossgate
South St.
N. Bailey
River Wear
Borough of Elvet
✝ St. Mary, N. Bailey
Barony of Elvet (Manor of Elvethall)
CATHEDRAL
St. Mary, S. Bailey ✝
S. Bailey
✝ St. Oswald's Church

0 yards 250

N

23 Anglo-Norman Durham.

top of which was encircled by its defensive wall. Just inside the wall along its eastern side ran the bailey, which contained the garrison quarters, where the castle guard had, as it were, 'house for duty' – at this time thirty-nine days a year military service. The civil population was served by two small churches, both dedicated to St Mary. The slopes of the peninsula were cleared of vegetation to reinforce its defence. Weirs across the river were the means of powering mills, besides deepening the water to add further to the defence.

Beyond the walled peninsula were four boroughs. Extending northwards was the Borough of Durham or Bishop's Borough; Framwellgate across the Wear and north of the Milneburn tributary was part of the same division. To the west and east of the peninsula were Crossgate and Elvet Boroughs, respectively. These were under the jurisdiction of the priory, having originally been given to the priory by Bishop William of St Calais from his palatinate estates. The fourth borough, that of St Giles or Gilesgate, grew up around the hospital of St Giles; after its destruction by Cumin, Bishop Le Puiset re-founded

St Godric (*c*.1065–1170) was born in Norfolk, and from a humble background became pedlar, then merchant and ship-owner – and, possibly, pirate – with extensive travels around the Mediterranean. In the early twelfth century he was converted by a visionary encounter with St Cuthbert, whose footsteps he was determined to follow. After a series of pilgrimages, not least to Jerusalem, he made his way to Durham and, after some time at the priory and working at the hospital church of St Giles, was granted permission in 1110 by Bishop Flambard to live as a hermit at Finchale, in part of the bishop's hunting forest, by the Wear 4 miles downriver from Durham.

He remained at Finchale for the rest of his life, at first with a rough timber chapel and shelter, and from 1115 with a small stone chapel. Here he took asceticism to extremes: he wore a hair shirt, went barefoot, slept on the ground and ate frugally. His knees were said to be hardened and horny with frequent kneeling; he would spend nights in prayer up to his neck in the river Wear.

Godric had an affinity with wild animals and gained a reputation for miracles and prophecy. Thomas Becket and Pope Alexander III are said to have sent emissaries to him for advice. He is best known for four poems, the oldest songs in England for which we have the original musical settings. (These songs were taught him in a vision by the Blessed Virgin Mary.)

He died in 1170, of great age, and was buried in his little stone chapel, which became the chancel of the church of a priory founded in 1196 but not completed until the mid-thirteenth century. It was a daughter-house of Durham and functioned as a holiday retreat for small groups of monks until the Dissolution. Today its extensive ruins in a sylvan setting are in the custodianship of English Heritage.

While our chief source of information on Durham's fourth saint comes from Godric's contemporary biographer, Reginald of Durham, the recent novel by Frederick Buecher, *Godric* (1981), evocatively recreates the life and times of the hermit.

the hospital in 1180 at Kepier and gave the borough to it as part of its estate. The remaining division was the Barony of Elvet or Manor of Elvethall, which had probably developed from early settlement in the vicinity of St Oswald's church, but which was now under the jurisdiction of the priory.

Stone-built churches were in the Market Place, Elvet, Crossgate and, less than a mile distant, at St Giles. Each was at the centre of its borough and formed the nucleus of settlements that remained distinctive, independent units.

A contemporary description of the city, probably composed in the monastery at Durham in the second half of the eleventh century,

24 Brother Laurence, prior and poet.

captures the particular combination of water, rock and building at the fortified centre. It constitutes the last extant Old English or Anglo-Saxon poem:

> This city is renowned throughout all Britain,
> set on steep slopes and marvellous built with
> rocks all round. A strongly running river
> flows past enclosed by weirs.[20]

The evident pride of place was repeated in a much longer composition, in Latin, a mere fifty years later by a Durham monk, Brother Lawrence, **(24)** who for the last five years of his life had been prior of the monastery. It has a similar opening: 'The ground rises up on high, a rocky plateau with rugged sides: sloping steeply in all directions it discourages an enemy, and moated by the river it mocks hostile forces. The rapid river envelopes it in the shape of a horse-shoe, a watery vale encircles the lofty place.'[21]

three

MEDIEVAL DURHAM

Walled Citadel

At the beginning of this period the fortified plateau was not only the core of Durham, it *was* Durham, for the various small boroughs around the centre, although under the jurisdiction of the bishop or prior, had evolved and functioned as separate units. From the citadel flowed the regional, indeed, national, political and ecclesiastical significance of the city. The prince-bishops, with their impressive palace and magnificent cathedral, were delegated regal powers in this northernmost part of the kingdom. They had an administrative system resembling that of the Crown, and were expected to be soldiers, besides being leader of the Church. While the cathedral contained within it the bishop's throne, it also contained, indeed was erected to house, the shrine of St Cuthbert, which was under the custodianship of the prior, head of the best endowed monastery in England.

The ecclesiastical renown and political eminence of the city were at their height a century or more before the dramatic changes ushered in by the Reformation. The civil settlement beyond the walls, meanwhile, remained throughout in the shadow of the ecclesiastical authorities. It was also more vulnerable to any Scottish foray into the area.

The Castle

The impregnable castle was increasingly embellished as the home of a succession of powerful bishops, most notably by Anthony Bek (bishop 1284–1310), Thomas Hatfield (1345–81), Richard Fox (1494–1501) and Cuthbert Tunstall (1530–59).

A new great hall was built by Bek above the Norman undercroft in the west range. It was enlarged by Hatfield, but subsequently truncated at the southern

end by Fox in order to insert kitchens and servery. The shortened hall still measured 35ft by 100ft, meaning that the Bishop of Durham dined in one of the finest great halls in the country. Had his guests inspected the kitchens, they would have been no less impressed by the ovens beneath magnificent low stone arches and castellated brickwork to the flues.

In front of the north range Tunstall built a two-storey gallery that linked to the great hall at one end and chapel at the other, both gallery and chapel being named after the bishop. To the east of the courtyard the octagonal keep was rebuilt in stone by Hatfield. Outside the castle gatehouse on Palace Green Bishop Neville (1437–57) built an exchequer, chancery and palatinate court. A bull's head crest of the bishop still projects from the building.

In terms of defence, the only access lacking protection from water was marked by an especially strong North Gate, which linked via a two-storey bastion to the keep. This was the work of Bishop Langley in the 1420s, who took the opportunity to use part of the gate as a prison, thereby releasing the cellars of the castle. To the castle walls there was added in the early fourteenth century a city wall enclosing a compact area, with the Market Place in the centre. Entry was defended by impressive gates and towers at the peninsula end of both bridges, and at Clayport and Walkergate.

The Cathedral

The most significant alteration to the cathedral in medieval times was the replacement of the modest apsidal east end with a more spacious eastern transept. Begun in 1242, its completion took almost forty years – almost as long as it took to build the cathedral itself. Earlier unsuccessful trials for erecting a lady chapel at the east end, together with the appearance of fractures, perhaps contributed to a greater depth of unconsolidated material here, resulting from the gentle easterly dip of the sandstone strata. It appears that the architect took advantage of this misfortune by incorporating a lower floor level as part of his design to create a taller, more spacious area in order to enhance the setting of the shrine of St Cuthbert. Height is further emphasised by the nine slender lancet windows and the fluted columns of Frosterley marble – a dark limestone from upper Weardale, which on close inspection is as much fossil as rock. The lancet windows were related to the additional chapels or altars for the saying of Mass. **(25)** Above, a large rose window was inserted.

25 The Chapel of Nine Altars.

The seamless attachment of the Early English transept onto the Romanesque cathedral was facilitated by the renewal of the high vault of the choir at the same time. Aesthetic reasons apart, there is little doubt that the more impressive setting for St Cuthbert's shrine was conceived in revenue-producing terms. Its initial funding was even partly achieved by the selling of indulgences, which freed contributors from thirty days' penance. It is possible that the idea of an expanded feretory with a circulatory area to replace the confined space of an apse may have had its origin long before the cathedral was finished. For, as mentioned in the previous chapter, in 1104, immediately preceding the translation of the saint to the completed east end, the body was inspected and found to be undecayed. Cuthbert, a miracle-worker in life, was evidently no ordinary saint in death, and therefore deserving perhaps of a prestigious setting.

Almost a century later the cathedral's most inspirational monument was erected: a canopied reredos screen between the high altar and shrine. The Neville screen, in celebration of the victory of Neville's Cross in 1346 and largely paid for by John Lord Neville, is composed of Caen stone from Normandy. It was designed by Henry Yevele, the leading mason of his time, and prefabricated in London, shipped to Newcastle and by cart to Durham, where it took seven masons nearly a year to erect. Sculptured figures of St Cuthbert and St Oswald flanked a standing Virgin in the centre of 107 painted and gilded statues. All the figures were removed at the Dissolution, but even today the skeletal effect of the vertical elements is quite remarkable. **(26)** It is the only surviving example of a canopied Perpendicular reredos of its kind in the country.

A third major change within the cathedral concerned the Galilee chapel. Between 1428 and 1435 Bishop Langley renewed the roof and added two sandstone columns to each of the paired columns of Purbeck marble. He also constructed new entrances to the nave either side of the cathedral's great west door, in front of which he placed his own chantry tomb. Outside the chapel Bishop Langley erected massive buttresses to stabilise its position on the very edge of the gorge.

Other changes were the conversion of many of the round-headed Romanesque windows to the pointed Gothic style – they were reinstated in the nineteenth century – and the renovation of the great west window. Unplanned were the necessary repairs to the central tower, the wooden spire of which was twice struck by lightning, the first time in 1429. The redesigned tower was not completed until 1490.

The impact of the cathedral on the medieval mind is not easy to imagine, although some insight is given in *The Rites of Durham*, an anonymous writing dated 1596, after the Reformation.[1] The writer was obviously familiar with the building, and looks back nostalgically to former days.

Apart from the overwhelming sense of space, the visitor's first impression was of colour. Red and black geometrical designs on the walls were further illuminated by light through the coloured glass that filled every window, not least the large windows in the west end and two transepts. The image of St Cuthbert dominated the windows: if the glazing of the cloisters is included, there were more than eighteen windows depicting various scenes of his life. [2] The nave had several separate chapels and altars, including the chantry of Ralph and Alice Neville, with his son John and his wife Maud nearby. Stretching between the two most forward pillars was the rood screen with the Jesus altar in front. Doors either side led to a stone choir screen, with one of the cathedral's three organs above. The view through the choir screen door was of the high altar and the stunning Neville screen with its coloured statues. On the south side, above the elaborate Hatfield chantry with its alabaster effigy, was the bishop's cathedra or throne, intentionally created to be the highest in Christendom: higher even than that of the Pope's in Rome. Doors either side of the high altar led through to St Cuthbert's shrine in the centre of a platform that jutted out into the Chapel of Nine Altars. The coffin rested on a

26 The Neville screen.

pedestal of green and gold marble, with a gilded and printed wooden cover with six bells, which rang whenever the cover was raised. Cupboards on either side contained an assortment of holy relics, among them a rib and milk of the Blessed Virgin Mary, the stone Christ sat on before Herod, a thorn from his crown worn at his Passion and a piece of the holy sepulchre. Beyond, each altar in the Chapel of Nine Altars had its own large partition and cover of colourful, gilded wainscot.

Notable among the adornments was the great Paschal Candle, which stood in the choir from Maunday Thursday to Ascension Day, and was said to reach as high as the triforium vaulting. Festivals must have been especially colourful, with monks in their fine copes led by the prior in a gold cope so heavy that he needed attendants on each side to support the weight.[3] From the late fourteenth century the prior also supported pontifical insignia as a result of the size of the monastic income.

According to *The Rites of Durham* the general opulence was such that the cathedral was 'accoumpted to be the richest churche in all this land ... so great was the rich Jewells, and ornaments, Copes, Vestments and plaite presented to holy St Cuthbert by Kinges, Queenes, Princes and Noblemen as is theis days is almost beyonde beleife'.[4]

The Monastery

The cathedral was, of course, an abbey church in which the daily and seasonal round of offices was kept by the Benedictine order while caring for the shrine of St Cuthbert. The abbey or monastery was also a hive of activity within its own complex of buildings immediately south of the cathedral, linked by a cloister arcade.

Extensive building or rebuilding continued during medieval times. Ample building stone remained relatively nearby, at Kepier and Baxter Wood. The extensive quarry to the west of South Street was now worked out and converted to an orchard and a series of controlled fish ponds for the abbey.[5] Several distinctive structures arose. Among the early reconstructions was that of the cloisters, provided for by Bishop Skirlaw (1388–1406). Along the north range, the sunny side, was a series of cubicles for study with tables or workbenches, the fixings of which can still be seen. Despite the arcade being glazed in, regular visits to a fire in a warming house would have been necessary in winter. There were also desks

in the dormitory cubicles. To the east was an impressive chapter house, where each day began with the office and reading of a chapter of the Benedictine Rule. The present chapter house is a reconstruction, the original having been pulled down during 'improvements' at the end of the eighteenth century.

The whole of the west range of the cloister, above the thirteenth-century warming house and former dormitory, was a new, enlarged dormitory for the increased number of monks. Built by master mason John de Middleton, it was completed in 1404. It runs the length of the west range, some 200ft, its width determined by the decision to retain the undercroft of the old sleeping quarters. Roofing was still a challenge, magnificently met in 40ft bulk oak timbers spanning the width, with arched braces and wall posts. It gives the appearance of an upturned hull of some mighty wooden galleon. **(27)** The layout of the monks' cubicles can be deduced from the arrangement of the tall Perpendicular windows.

On the south range was the refectory, standing forward of which was a remarkable octagonal building, the monastic kitchen (also known as the prior's or great kitchen). Completed in 1374 and designed by John Lewyn, principal mason to the abbey, the complex interlacing ribs of its vault are unlike anything else in England. **(28)** Perhaps the tenth-century *maqsurah* of the Great Mosque at Cordoba inspired the designer.

27 The monks' dormitory.

The sixteenth-century gatehouse, with St Helen's chapel above, and the entry from the bailey, is a third extant building of note from this period. The Prior's Lodging, of which today only the lower courses are detectable in the present Deanery, were luxurious quarters to which were attached a chapel and hall. The range of other buildings – guesthouse, infirmary, offices, granary, brewhouse, barns, stables, reredorter, even a 'lying house' (a prison for monks who had committed a serious offence) – today require the eye of faith to detect. While all may not have been architectural gems or glamorous, all were integral parts of the highly varied and complex operation that constituted the monastery. **(29)**

The number of monks resident in the medieval abbey varied between fifty and seventy, except for the years immediately following the Black Death of 1349 when half fell victim to the plague. Apart from the daily round, study and instruction constituted an important element in Benedictine life. This was furthered from the late thirteenth century by sending brethren to Oxford to spend time in a house that was to become known as Durham College. In the mid-fourteenth century Bishop Bury (1333–45) founded a college library, which at the time was considered by some to be the finest collection of books in England. A measure

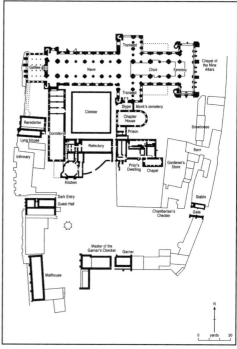

28 Vaulting in the great kitchen.

29 The abbey.

of its importance was that there were no fewer than five keepers to oversee the collection. Bishop Hatfield, successor to Bishop Bury, further extended the college. By this time one-third of all Durham monks spent a period at the college, while all priors had long been its 'graduates'.

The Benedictine rule of hospitality was evident in its school for poor children and rooms for elderly women by the gatehouse, while attached to the Langley chantry was a school to teach grammar and song to poor children. There was also a font in the Galilee chapel to baptise children of excommunicated parents.

Hospitality of a different nature and scale might be seen when the simple, ordinary round was punctuated by festival celebration. They may still have been basking in the victory at the Battle of Neville's Cross, but the cellarer's list of provisions for Whitsunday 1347 is perhaps a window on a quality of festive living:

600 Salt Herrings	Fish
9 Oxen carcases salted	3 Kids
400 White Herrings	5 stones Hog's Lard
2½ Oxen fresh	71 Geese
55 Cod	4 stones Cheese, Butter, Milk
1 Oxen carcase fresh	59 Chicken
30 Salted Salmon	Pottle of Vinegar and Honey
14 Calves	14 Capons
14 Ling	14 pounds Figs and Raisons
7½ Swine carcases in salt	60 Pigeons
4 Turbot	13 pounds Almonds
6 Swine carcases fresh	1300 Eggs
2 horseloads White Fish	8 pounds Rice
26 Suckling Porkers	Pepper, Saffron, Cinnamon, Other
Plaice, Sparlings, Eels, Freshwater	Spices

The monastic kitchen had regularly to feed some 2–300 a day, for the monks were far outnumbered by all kinds of craftsmen, tradesmen and servants. The range of business tasks conducted is indicated by the fact that the monks had to fill some twenty different offices. Not the least of these operations was managing the priory's lands and estates and collecting rents and tithes. Income from this most important source of revenue, which originally derived from its lands of the patrimony of St Cuthbert, had been increased through time by benefactors giving further property and by appropriation of various churches. Under the latter act, vicars were installed in appropriated parishes with a low income, the bulk of the revenue going to the priory.

More obvious sources of revenue were donations, offerings and sale of indulgences. A further general source was the so-called 'Peter's Pence', whereby since 1164 the priory could collect a penny from every household of the diocese; in addition, donations were expected from the required annual visit to the cathedral. The abbey was also periodically enriched every time a bishop died, when a host of valuable goods and chattels were received. One indication of the wealth of the priory might be the 'loan' to which impecunious Henry VI helped himself in 1448. This was never repaid.

It is perhaps only to be expected that the prior of such a well-endowed institution might exhibit an appropriate lifestyle. Beyond the priory he was conveyed in an impressive carriage with an attendant entourage. One prior was noted for scattering specially minted coins from his carriage. He also had a summer residence at Beaurepaire (Bearpark), 2 miles west of Durham, set in a deer park of more than 1,300 acres, one of the biggest in England.

Bishop-Priory Relations

The monastery at Durham enjoyed its most prosperous period in the second half of the fourteenth century and first half of the fifteenth. This period not only coincided with outstanding priors and bishops, but is also notable for the fact that the latter not only devoted much attention to the cathedral but equally worked in harmony with the priory. Harmonious relations were not always present during the medieval period.

The constitution of the priory had been drawn up by Bishop William of St Calais, who was also responsible for dividing the estates belonging to the old community between bishop and priory. Under the constitution the bishop was abbot of the priory, and therefore superior to the prior. The latter, however, was the *de facto* head of the priory in practice if not out of necessity, for, apart from long inter-regna, bishops could be absent for long periods, even for years in some instances. Moreover, bishops were rarely monks, sometimes not even people who exhibited obvious spiritual values. They were, rather, administrators, diplomats and courtiers. Several were Lord or High Chancellor of England, or treasurer or secretary to the king. Little wonder, therefore that the Bishop of Durham should have his own house or palace in London.

Under the constitution the monks were eligible to elect their bishop – a few emerged from their own brethren – but the Crown's nomination was to be known before the election. Elections, moreover, brought a recurring dilemma: although a strong bishop was a welcomed counter in disputes with the Archbishop of York over metropolitan rights, such a bishop might also hold strong opinions that did not conform to those of the monastic community. The two parties could well therefore be in dispute. Bishop Anthony Bek is the clearest example of such confrontation.

Anthony Bek was Bishop of Durham from 1284 to 1310. There can be no doubt as to his power and influence. During his career he was chief adviser to the king and the monarch's diplomat in half a dozen foreign courts; he also held the title of Patriarch of Jerusalem. He accompanied the king to Scotland in 1298, where he led the siege of Dirleton Castle before leading his large retinue (under the banner of St Cuthbert) of standard bearers, knights, cavalry and infantrymen at the victorious battle at Falkirk. The complaint of the last-named that they were only obliged to defend the patrimony of St Cuthbert, that is the land between the rivers Tyne and Tees, was made to no effect.

The bishop's power was matched by his legendary wealth. The magnificence of his entourage to Rome is said to have impressed even the Pope. At home there is a story relating to a roll of cloth that a London merchant reportedly boasted was too expensive even for the Bishop of Durham. Bek's response was to purchase it, and to cut it in pieces as covers for his horses.

The Prior of Durham, then, must initially have been encouraged when, immediately after his consecration at York, Bek refused the archbishop's request that he excommunicate the Prior of Durham and his monks. The archbishop was still sore from having been refused entry to the cathedral a few months earlier. However, on arrival in Durham, Bek declined to meet the prior's welcoming party and refused the right of the prior to enthrone him. He then went further, removing both prior and sub-prior, and brought back from retirement an elderly former prior. When the latter died four years later, and the monks elected a new prior, Richard of Hoton, administering the priory became a difficult or near-impossible task. In the end the prior was forced to appeal to the Pope by travelling to Rome, despite the bishop's best efforts to prevent him leaving Durham. Prior Hoton won his case, but unfortunately died on the return journey. It was therefore his successor who was to experience the change in attitude by, and generosity of, the bishop, such that on his death Anthony Bek became the first bishop to be buried in the cathedral. Previous bishops had been interred in the chapter house.

Urban Boroughs

Beyond the fortified citadel the several small independent communities had slowly expanded within their boroughs. Although all were under the jurisdiction or overlordship of the priory or bishop, each was self-contained, with its own church (except New Elvet), courthouse (for paying rents and settling disputes), guildhall, and mill and bakehouse (both of which tenants were obliged to use). There was, therefore, 'little local appreciation of Durham as a single urban area, a town in its own right, through most of the medieval period'.[6]

Despite the lack of administrative unity, the overall settlement pattern had been laid down during the Anglo-Norman period, with its distinctive core and half-a-dozen streets leading into the countryside. During the medieval period there was a continuous line of housing in Sadlergate and Fleshergate linking the peninsula with the Market Place, and in both Claypath and Silver Street leading from the Market Place, also immediately across the two bridges in New Elvet and Crossgate. **(30)**

The locational advantage of Bishop's Borough, in the shadow of the castle and at the meeting of the three main roads into Durham, is evident. The Market Place was the focal point: the commercial hub; the urban heart. A guildhall was built here by Bishop Hatfield in 1356. No other borough possessed a market; indeed, the bishop refused to grant one to New Elvet. The concentration of activity about the Market Place is signified by the occupational street names that were found here and nowhere else – Sadlergate (leather workers), Fleshergate (butchers), Silver Street (jewellers), Souterpeth (shoemakers) and Walkergate (clothworkers). (The suffix -gate is derived from Old Norse, *geata*, for street.) Shops, stalls and booths characterised the central area, and later clustered at the west end of Framwellgate Bridge and on the multi-arched Elvet Bridge.[7]

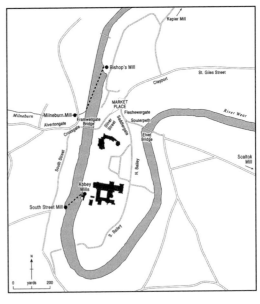

30 Medieval Durham: streets and mills.

The Market Place gained a further significant municipal facility in the mid-fifteenth century when a public water supply was provided. A central pant was fed by conduit from Fram Well Head in Sidegate, on the west side of the river, through the generosity of Thomas Billingham of nearby Crook Hall. Elsewhere wells were the source of water, including on the peninsula, where bands of impervious shale beneath the sandstone gave rise to a perched watertable. The Market Place and vicinity was also one of the few areas likely to have been paved; elsewhere the norm would have been trodden earth and ash, fronted by single-storeyed wooden and wattle and daub dwellings.

The presence of running water determined other activities, most obviously the eight mills, but also for a tanning industry on the west bank of the Wear or its tributary, the Milneburn, in Crossgate Borough. Although lacking potential as a navigable waterway, the Wear, given its wide catchment area in the Pennines, was still able to wreak damage from flooding. Mills were especially vulnerable. Scaltok Mill in Elvet was damaged several times before finally being abandoned in the mid-fifteenth century. Again, the vulnerability of many of the dwellings in low-lying New Elvet occasioned the building of a wall as a barrier. Framwellgate Bridge itself was destroyed in a severe flood at the beginning of the fifteenth century. It was rebuilt by Bishop Langley, with the two wide elliptical arches that we recognise today. A century later the burden of repair on the bishop was eased by the sale of indulgences. Both bridges were valuable as a source of income, not only from tolls but from the booths that crowded on their structures. From the late thirteenth century Elvet Bridge also incorporated chantry chapels – St Andrew at the lower end and St James at the peninsular end.

The picture to emerge of medieval Durham, then, is that, despite its ecclesiastical and political significance, as a civil settlement it remained very much under the dominance of the ecclesiastical authorities, a small market town with a limited hinterland. The summary of the most detailed study of this period concluded that 'Durham remained in a state of "arrested development" to the end of the middle ages, with its ecclesiastical overlords making no concessions on self-government'.[8]

Despite the dominance just described, the lack of any real independence does not appear to have sparked any movement for self-government. Several convincing reasons for this pacificity have been put forward.[9] Firstly, the ecclesiastical masters appear to have been neither oppressive nor unjust. Craft unions developed late, while the professional class served the authorities. There was a common interest, moreover, in servicing the church authorities and pilgrim trade, while all shared a pride in being Cuthbert's people and in having his shrine in their great cathedral. An annual event that illustrated this concord was the Corpus Christi Day procession, when the trade guilds, carrying the Sacrament from the Corpus Christi shrine in St Nicholas's, preceded by the banners and congregations of the churches in Durham, went in procession to Palace Green, where they were met by the prior and monks with the banner of St Cuthbert. The procession then continued into the cathedral for a joint service and a pilgrimage to the shrine of St Cuthbert. After returning to St Nicholas's the day was rounded off by mystery plays in the Market Place, performed by guild members.

The Auld Enemy

From time to time the authorities and townsfolk of Durham were made aware of their border position close to Scotland. Although the river Tweed had been accepted as the boundary between the two countries from the mid-twelfth century, relations between England and Scotland still swung between amicability and animosity. Situated astride the main north-south route, it was inevitable that Durham was affected by events that had their origins elsewhere. The late thirteenth century and first half of the fourteenth was a particularly unsettled period.

In 1296 Edward I intervened in the king-making of Scotland, eventually making himself overlord and returning south with the symbolic Stone of Scone. The response was a Scottish uprising and victory over an English force at Stirling Bridge under William Wallace, who then pursued the enemy as far as the outskirts of Durham, whence storms, cold and hunger brought about a retreat. The intervention of St Cuthbert was seen in this. The event brought Edward I north again in 1298, together with his adviser on Scotland, Bishop Anthony Bek, and the bishop's large retinue. The Scots were comprehensively defeated.

Durham, however, was to pay for this glorious episode with almost two decades of threat and interference. Edward I died without resolving the Scottish constitutional troubles, which were left to his weak son, Edward II. Anthony Bek had also died. Edward's force was defeated at Bannockburn in 1314 by Robert the Bruce, who like his predecessor again marched south as far as Durham, which he briefly held before the city managed to buy itself out. In

1315 the townspeople successfully petitioned for a wall to protect that part of the Bishop's Borough around the Market Place. Accordingly a rectangular area was enclosed north of the castle walls, with gates at Framwellgate Bridge, Walkergate, Clayport and Elvet Bridge. (31) The new defence, or town wall, was not as strong as the castle walls and, of course, offered no protection to the other boroughs. Scottish incursions were by now a regular occurrence, and the city more than once paid for truces, whereby Scottish forces might pass unmolested through the palatinate if the city were bypassed. Little wonder, therefore, that 'Scotsman' should become a term of abuse, or that persons from across the border were prevented from joining guilds.

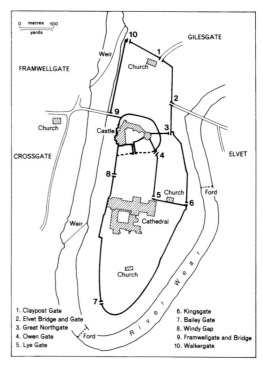

31 Medieval Durham: walls and gates.

The Battle of Neville's Cross

In 1346 there occurred the most notable incursion to focus on Durham. Edward III was now king, and had embarked on an invasion of France in what was to become the protracted series of conflicts we know as the Hundred Years War. In August 1346 Edward defeated the French at Crécy, whereupon Philip IV invoked the Franco-Scottish Treaty by appealing to David II of Scotland to invade England in order to divert attention and relieve pressure on his forces. David therefore marched south with, perhaps, some 12,000 men, fortified by the knowledge that the bulk of the English troops were in France. In response, the Archbishop of York gathered a force principally through the assistance of noblemen Henry Percy of Northumberland, Ralph Neville of Durham and Thomas Rokeby, sheriff of Yorkshire. The Bishop of Durham, Bishop Hatfield, was with Edward on his French expedition. The probable size of the assembled force was 6,000.

The invaders camped at Beaurepaire on 16 October, on the eve of what became known as the Battle of Neville's Cross. The two armies were each arranged in three 'battles' or divisions and were in position by nine in the morning, although battle did not commence until the afternoon. It was fought out on the open ground of Beaurepaire Moor, and especially on the narrow north-south ridge of the Browney-Wear watershed of Crossgate Moor. **(32)** The crucial factor that contributed to the English victory was probably the fire-power of their archers. This, together with the steeply sloping terrain, worked to the disadvantage of the initial strategy of the Scots when their west wing decided to attack. Their east wing then fell prey to the archers of the Percy-Neville division. The retreat of both then allowed all three English divisions to concentrate on the central division led by King David. It ended with the invading force finally routed and the capture of King David, who had been wounded in the battle.

The story of Durham's most famous battle would be incomplete without mention of the role of St Cuthbert, who appeared to both sides. King David ignored the request that he should not invade the saint's territory, while Prior Fosser obeyed his advice to take the Holy Corporax (the precious relic found in Cuthbert's coffin and used to cover the holy sacrament), put it on a spear and carry it to the battlefield at Redhills. Thus did the prior and attendants kneel in prayer on a mound known as Maiden's Bower, a Bronze Age barrow in Flass Vale, while the battle raged. Other monks, who are said to have watched the battle from the top of the cathedral tower, will have had a better, if more distant, view of the proceedings.

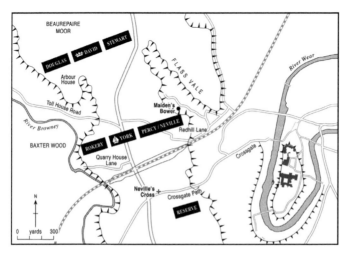

32 The Battle of Neville's Cross.

Afterwards the whole brethren assembled in the cathedral to give thanks, returning the precious relic, which was joined by the Scottish Black Rood (a reliquary in the shape of a cross, carrying part of the True Cross), symbol of that country's identity.

Its exact provenance is uncertain, perhaps captured in battle and a gift from Ralph Neville, or perhaps a gift from Edward III as a thank-offering. What is certain is that King David spent eleven years in the Tower of London, while Prior Fosser is reported to have rejoiced at the 'bringing to an end the pitiful discord which prevailed between the English and Scots over the course of many years'.[10]

One final point about the battle is its name. Although it took place little more than a mile from the city, and although there was at the time no settlement of Neville's Cross, there was a cross of that name, which stood as a waymarker at a crossing of two ancient routeways. From the west, and passing Brancepeth Castle, home of the Nevilles who had been in the county since the twelfth century, was a route of at least Roman origin that entered the city less than a mile distant via Framwellgate Bridge. (It is possible that the name of the present road, and that of the prior's borough which it traverses – both 'Crossgate' – may be derived from the waymarker.) The second route runs north-south along the narrow ridge between the rivers Wear and Browney on the alignment of the Roman road to Chester-le-Street.

The Neville family presumably erected the initial waymarker. After the battle Lord Ralph Neville replaced it with an elaborate stone cross, 25ft high, richly carved and presumably painted. While still a waymarker, it now stood very near the battleground as a commemoration of victory. Forty years later a second celebration of the victory was erected, the gift this time of Lord John Neville in the form of the Neville screen in the cathedral. The celebratory cross features in *The Rites of Durham* and is clearly shown on Speed's map of 'Bishoprick and Citie of Durham' of 1611. It is now imprisoned behind railings with only the socket or base of the octagonal shaft considered to be original. A scholarly review of historical sources has enabled Martin Roberts to produce a likely reconstruction of the celebratory cross.[11] **(33)**

A more permanent allusion to the battle is recorded in Shakespeare's *Henry V*.

Near to the end of the Hundred Years War, the English king again finds himself in France about to do battle with the French. In Act I, scene ii, Henry says to the Archbishop of Canterbury:

33 Neville's Cross: a suggested reconstruction and today.

For you shall read that my great-grandfather
Never went with his forces into France
But that the Scot on his unfurnish'd kingdom
Came pouring, like the tide into a breach,
With ample and brim fullness of his force,
Galling the gleaned land with hot essays,
Girding with grievous siege castles and towns;
That England, being empty of defence,
Hath shook and trembled at the ill neighbourhood.'
But the Archbishop replies:
'She hath been then more fear'd than harm'd my liege;
For hear her but exampled by herself:
When all her chivalry hath been in France,
And she a mourning widow of her nobles,
She hath herself not only well defended,
But taken, and impounded as a stray,
The king of Scots; whom she did send to France,
To fill Edward's fame with prisoner kings'

Beaurepaire, 'beautiful retreat', was the summer residence of the priors of Durham little more than 2 miles from the city. It was in the centre of an estate of over 1,300 acres on the northern bank of the river Browney. An initial gift of 100 acres by Gilbert de la Lay of Witton in 1154 was considerably augmented during the first half of the thirteenth century by a series of gifts to the priory, largely from bishops of Durham.

Prior Bertram of Middleton (1244–58) built the first retreat, consisting of residence and chapel. Subsequent priors added a series of buildings, including dormitory and dining hall. Outside was a series of fishponds, while cattle and game were kept in the extensive park, which was first enclosed in 1257, initially with fencing, replaced by a stone wall in 1311. The wall is prominently shown on Speed's map in the early seventeenth century.

Beaurepaire was not only attractive, it was also isolated and thus vulnerable to Scottish forays into the area. In 1315 the cattle and game were destroyed by a Scottish force; in 1346 King David did likewise, laying waste to the park before the Battle of Neville's Cross. Much later, in the 1640s, the Scottish army completed the destruction of the buildings. (Much earlier, quarrelsome Bishop Bek (1284–1310), during a dispute with the monastery, is recorded as having broken down the fence and driven out the game.)

After the Dissolution the park was granted to the Dean and Chapter, who subsequently administered it as an estate of tenant farmers. More recently, between 1872 and 1984, there was an interlude when coal was extracted from a series of seams beneath the estate by the Bearpark Coal and Coke Company. By this time Bearpark had become the accepted corruption of the Norman-French name. Today all obvious evidence of the colliery has disappeared, but ruins on the bank of the Browney, adjacent to Bearpark Hall Farm, still bare witness to its earlier history

four

DURHAM REFORMED

I f the medieval period in Durham is perceived as an essentially evolution-
ary time, albeit with interruptions by Scottish incursions or inflictions
of 'pestilences', there followed a period that brought abrupt and lasting change. Renaissance ideas arriving from the continent gave rise to
opposing factions within the Church, which, together with Henry VIII's marital
manoeuvring, led to a re-evaluation of Church-State relations. Although the
agents of change were in London and the South, their influence in terms of
policy – and through personnel dispatched to the more conservative North
– was to bring to an end Durham's centuries-old form of ecclesiastical organisation and worship. The same forces also brought about a re-evaluation of the
city's strategic regional role within the national picture.

Dissolution of the Monastery

Although on the eve of the Dissolution the Benedictine order still revered the
body of their saint – in the words of Moorhouse, 'Durham's patron saint and
the raison d'etre of its monastery still ran the Almighty pretty close when it
came to adoration and awe'[1] – pilgrims no longer flocked to the shrine. In the
South, moreover, monasteries themselves were no longer held in high esteem
but often regarded rather as centres of relic worship and superstition. At the
same time many still owned large estates and wielded considerable power. The
reputed wealth of Durham certainly made it especially vulnerable to any would-
be reformers of the system, such as that led on behalf of the king by Thomas
Cromwell, the Lord Privy Seal.

   The first move came in 1536 when religious houses with incomes below £200
were suppressed. Durham thereby lost its outlying cells, except for Durham
College. When two commissioners inspected the mother-house at Durham no

irregularities were found, which was not the case in some other monasteries. The commissioners also searched the palaces of Bishop Tunstall at Auckland and Durham. Then, in 1538, three commissioners of Henry VIII arrived in search of the monastery's valuables.

The search was thorough to the extent that all coffins were opened, including the elevated shrine coffin of St Cuthbert. The latter required a sledgehammer, and one of the saint's legs was broken. When the perpetrator informed his colleagues that it was not possible to throw down the broken limb as requested because 'ye synewes and ye skin held it', the others ascended the ladder in order to be convinced. They ordered that the body be kept safe until the king's pleasure was known and, after breaking up Cuthbert's elaborate shrine, left with their hoard.

The fact that Durham experienced minimal physical destruction during the suppression of its monastery is not a little attributable to the wisdom and moderate disposition – and, perhaps, instinct for self-preservation – of both Bishop Cuthbert Tunstall and Prior Hugh Whitehead. The former, who earlier had to make good the neglect by Wolsey, considered it expedient to accept Henry's claim to be Supreme Head of the Church, although naturally conservative or traditional in religious matters. As president of the King's Council in the North Parts, he would have been embarrassed by the majority view of members who sympathised with the Pilgrimage of Grace, but evaded responsibility, and avoided any culpability, by diplomatically retiring to his residence on the Tweed at Norham during this episode.

Prior Whitehead, who had wisely led the monastery since 1524, officially surrendered its buildings and estates in December 1538 and awaited the outcome. It arrived in 1541 when Letters Patent re-founded the institution as the Cathedral Church of Christ and the Virgin Mary, Cuthbert being dropped from the designation. There was to be a ruling body of a dean and chapter of twelve prebendaries, and a further twelve minor canons. Endowment came with the return of the former abbey's estates, but with an annual charge payable to London.

Change was therefore accompanied by continuity, continuity in both buildings and personnel – the latter emphasised in the appointment of Whitehead as the first dean. Again, although the Benedictine order had been disbanded, the style of worship remained what might be described as non-papal Catholicism, a fact partly attributable to its position in the conservative North, but more to the fact that in the 1540s two exclusively defined parties of Catholic and Protestant had yet to crystallise. In Trevelyan's words, 'opinion was in the making, not yet formed'.[2] A decade later, however, opinions had hardened and could literally be a matter of life and death as the relationship between Church and State underwent a series of twists and turns. There was more to the Reformation than the Dissolution of the Monasteries.

Years of Turmoil

By the early 1550s Dean Whitehead had died, and Bishop Tunstall had been deprived of his see during the regency of Edward VI. In their place Protestant leaders were dispatched to Durham. English, and the 1552 Prayer Book, replaced Latin, although, as Shanks remarks, 'to the great number of Durham people who used a broad Northumbrian dialect, Cranmer's literary English must have been hardly more understandable, and much less familiar in sound, than the old language'.[3] What would certainly have been noticed was puritan Dean Horne's removal of all stained glass and decorative features from the cathedral.

Then in 1553 Mary ascended to the English throne. As a consequence Bishop Tunstall was reinstated and Dean Horne was replaced by a Catholic dean. Latin Mass also returned, and was largely welcomed by both clergy and laity. However, Mary in turn was soon superseded by Elizabeth, so the pendulum swung yet again. Bishop Tunstall lost his see once more. Although he had been prudent enough to distance himself from Mary's vengeful burnings, he felt unable to assent to Elizabeth's Act of Supremacy (abolishing papal powers) and Act of Uniformity. The dean was similarly removed.

Two leaders sympathetic to the Protestant cause were appointed. Dean Horne was reinstated and Bishop Pilkington became the first Protestant bishop of Durham. The former soon moved on, but his replacement, Dean Whittingham, proved even more zealous. According to *Rites*, 'he could not abyde anye godlie Religiousness or monasticall life'.[4] All idolatrous statues, carvings and brasses were removed or defaced; holy water stoups were put to use in stables; superstitious books were burnt. To complete the cleansing, the whole of the interior of the cathedral was lime-washed. The dean's wife joined in the Puritan cleansing by burning the sacred Banner of St Cuthbert.

Such rampant, iconoclastic Puritanism offended not only many clergy but also many landowners and commoners, to the extent that in 1569 there was a second northern uprising to restore Catholicism and the Latin Mass. Led by the Catholic feudal chiefs – primarily Charles Neville, Earl of Westmorland and Thomas Percy, Earl of Northumberland – they entered Durham, tore up the English Bible and Prayer Book and forced the clergy to celebrate the Mass according to the old order. Although the bulk of citizens were probably sympathetic to the cause and willing participants in the events, which centred on the cathedral,[5] there was no support further south – where there was no wish to join what was seen as a rebellion on behalf of Mary against Elizabeth. The Rising of the North therefore disintegrated, its leaders fled and 800 were executed, sixty of them in Durham, some by means more excruciating than hanging. Thomas Percy was executed in York; Charles Neville escaped abroad to live in exile. The castle homes of the Nevilles at Brancepeth and Raby, where the rebellion had been planned, were confiscated, as was their townhouse in the centre of the city, with its extensive grounds in Claypath extending down to the river. (William Wordsworth records many of these events in his long narrative poem *The White Doe of Rylstone*.)

In terms of what had gone before there now followed a relatively quieter period. Two of the deans were actually laymen, neither of whom found it necessary to visit Durham. In 1620, when the fourteen years of the lay deans ended, the new appointee, Richard Hunt, came from Cambridge and introduced other churchmen, not least John Cosin in 1624. At this time the ritual side of worship was increased by episcopal command of the Archbishop of Canterbury. In the cathedral Cosin led the way with all the trappings of high Anglicanism. The communion table, which had been placed in the centre of the choir, was replaced in the east end as an altar; the choir itself was painted and gilded; music, ritual and vestments returned. This was not, however, universally welcomed by the Chapter. One prebendary preached an outspoken sermon in which he berated 'superstitious vanities, ceremonial fooleries, apish toys, and popish trinkets'.[6] High Anglicanism, however, was supported by Charles I, who also stopped persecution of Roman Catholics, and Cosin was well known at Court. (He had been master of ceremonies at the king's coronation.)

Charles I, however, was to prove vulnerable when he adopted the role of absolute monarch, such that the overall context of reformation broadened to incorporate Parliament at the centre. As a consequence the church at Durham was again to experience dramatic change.

In 1640, after the king had failed to impose his will on Scotland, an ill-prepared English army was defeated at Newburn on Tyne. Durham suffered from

Ecclesiæ Cath Dunelmenſis,
facies Septentrionalis,

The North Prospect of the Cathedral
Church of Durham.

Daniel King delin: et sculpsit

34 The north front of Durham Cathedral by Daniel King, 1655.

looting by the retreating English forces, which was every bit as thorough as that of the following Scots who occupied the city for two years. The 'Army of the Covenant' was able to set its own terms for withdrawal. Eventually Parliament bought the Scots out of the northern counties. During their stay they had confiscated the revenue of the cathedral in order to maintain their forces. They also damaged some contents of the building, notably the font and organ, but such action was to pale into significance at the end of the decade when Cromwell used the cathedral as a prison to hold 2–3,000 Scots captured at the battle of Dunbar. All woodwork was destroyed, besides, not surprisingly, that of the Neville chantry and mutilation of the effigy of the victor of Neville's Cross. The prison hospital for the captives was in the castle, a use hardly conducive to the care of the building.

When Charles I lost the Civil War and his battle with Parliament, there followed eleven years of parliamentary rule during the Commonwealth. The king was eventually executed. Durham's heart stopped beating when the bishopric was abolished in 1646 and its lands sold. Three years later the Dean and Chapter were abolished and their lands also sold. At the same time the castle was confiscated and sold to the Lord Mayor of London. The result was that for the next decade the cathedral and former monastery buildings were neglected and vandalised. The cathedral had a leaking roof, no glass in its windows and

was without any woodwork. In the 1650s even the lead-covered timber spires on the west turrets were dismantled and the materials sold. The spires are shown in the drawing engraved by Daniel King in 1655, immediately before their removal. **(34)** In the former priory precinct all but one of the prebendary houses fell into ruin, while lead was stolen from the guest house with disastrous consequences. There was no use for the former agricultural buildings, anyway, since the working community had long since departed. A low point had been reached in the story of Durham.

Restoration

Eventually, in 1660, a British compromise saw the Crown, Parliament and Episcopacy restored together. Charles II was invited to accept the crown, and who should play a central role in his coronation but John Cosin, who had been equally prominent at the coronation of Charles I. Cosin, who had been in France for seventeen years to escape impeachment by Parliament, was made Bishop of Durham, along with a fellow Royalist as dean. The latter was soon recalled to restore St Paul's, but his successor, John Sudbury, and the bishop rapidly set about restoring the complex set of ecclesiastical buildings. The contribution of Cosin, who spent much of his own wealth in the process, has proved to be a remarkable and lasting imprint. He was one of Durham's great prince-bishops. **(35)**

The cathedral was made watertight and enriched by exuberantly carved choir screen and organ case, choir stalls, massive litany desk and a 40ft-high font cover, all in a combination of Gothic and Baroque sensibilities that we sum-marise today as 'Cosin woodwork'. In practice, of course, it is a tribute to the craftsmanship of a few talented local carpenters and joiners whom he engaged. The same woodwork is readily recog-nised in the castle in one of the most impressive staircases of its kind in England.[7] **(36)** Its carved dark balustrade panels rise through four floors in a square stairwell. Moreover, it was originally free-standing, being cantilevered from the walls.

35 Bishop John Cosin, Prebend of Durham 1624–43, Bishop of Durham 1660–72.

Later sagging, when an additional storey was added, required the insertion of rounded trunks resting on Tuscan-style newel posts. The corner turret with its staircase was the crucial circulation point linking the floors of the north and west ranges of the castle.

At the end of the north range Cosin extended Tunstall's chapel; on the west range he restored the great hall after replacement of the lead that had been stripped from the roof. Over the great hall door from the courtyard he built a protecting portico in classical style, flanked by buttresses topped by cupolas. The stone was obtained from Broken Walls Quarry, between the Galilee chapel and castle – a surprisingly late instance of quarrying on the riverbanks.[8] Through such additions and luxurious furnishings the castle became again a palace fit for a prince-bishop.

Outside, Cosin developed several castle ornamental gardens to complement the gracious living within. A garden constructed in the courtyard had as its central feature a fountain 14ft high. Most ambitious was the shaping of the motte into a triple set of terraces. The garden known as Bishop's Walk, running in a strip parallel to the river, suggests that the defensive function of the castle wall was no longer the primary concern. Indeed, changes in the methods of warfare resulting from the introduction of gunpowder would have lessened its protective value anyway.

36 Black staircase, Durham Castle.

On the east side of Palace Green Cosin re-founded Bishop Langley's almshouses, with rooms at either end for schools (1666); on the west side, on the site of the castle's stables, next to the exchequer and chancery court, he built a 'public library' for clergy, gentry and scholars (1669). Its interior consists entirely of wall shelving, as opposed to right-angled book shelving, being second only to the Bodleian Library in this country to adopt what was the continental manner. Cosin had been a keen book collector all his career, and was assiduous in their cataloguing and maintenance. The stipend for the library keeper, for instance, was to include the cost of rubbing each book in front of a fire at least once a month during the winter months to prevent mould.[9] It can be no surprise that the bishop-scholar should put over the door the motto, in Latin, 'Not the least part of learning is familiarity with good books'. The collection, which was valuable from the very beginning, soon included Cosin's annotated copy of his corrections and suggestions for inclusion in the 1662 Book of Common Prayer. **(37)** His influence in the finished book is to be seen not only in the prayers but also in the fact that he has the only hymn to be included; it has been sung at the ordination of all priests in the Church of England since 1662. On the national stage, therefore, Cosin played a prominent role in a project that was designed to re-

37 Bishop Cosin's handwritten annotations to the draft of the 1662 Book of Common Prayer.

establish 'reasonable' religion, part of a concerted effort to restore English life to the stability known before the Civil War and Commonwealth.

Bishop Cosin was also widely active in the diocese, with at least a dozen church buildings and their furnishings attributed to him and his associates. He also restored his palace of Auckland Castle, alongside which he added a large chapel, and fought for the return of Durham House as his London palace.

Dean John Sudbury played his part in restoring the cathedral and key buildings of the former monastery, notably enlarging the premises for the collection of books on the site of the former refectory and reconstructing the minor canons' houses. Thus, the buildings in the monastic precincts, which had formerly contained a series of agricultural units and workshops, were gradually adapted to other uses.

Cosin was succeeded by Bishop Nathaniel Crewe, described by diarist Pepys after a visit to Durham in 1682 as a bishop who 'seems to live more like a prince of this than a preacher of the other world'.[10] From his diaries it would appear that Pepys was a frequent diner at the bishop's table in London. Crewe's long episcopate owed much to a sublimation of conscience: in his ability to switch allegiance from courting James II to William of Orange[11] – even though his conscience initially caused him to flee the country on the overthrow of King James. Bishop notwithstanding, the restored order and dignity at the cathedral and its services continued. On her visit Celia Fiennes was surprised and impressed by the finery of the embroidered copes worn by the dean and prebendaries – 'the only place they use such things in England, and several more ceremonies and rites retained from the times of popery'.[12]

The heart of Durham was certainly beating again.

The Post-Medieval City

In the shadow of the peninsula's core, to which it was politically and commercially linked, the small feudal settlement below inevitably shared in its fortunes and misfortunes, including those causes that might arise far from Durham. Moreover, with regard to forays from across the Scottish border, it was more susceptible to disruption than the core, for although the centre had been surrounded by a town wall since the early fourteenth century, the defences lacked the additional protection of precipitous river banks afforded by the castle walls. The aftermath of the Rising of the North also brought impoverishment to the area through the loss of many of the land-owning – and, therefore, managing – class. Plagues or 'pestilences' further exacerbated conditions. During the severe plague of 1598 all who could leave fled the city, with the poor camping in makeshift huts on the surrounding moors. It claimed more than 800 lives, between a quarter and a third of the total population.

Meanwhile, the gradual decline in pilgrimage, and then closure of the monastery, meant that the part of the town economy dependent on, or connected with, its fairs and festivals and catering for the visitor no longer brought prosperity. The destruction of the Corpus Christi shrine and the suppression of its guild, around which much of the activity centred, was an additional blow. As the pilgrimage trade declined, however, an increasing number of trades, with their guilds, gradually emerged. Small-scale manufacturing, much of it for local consumption, was beginning.

In 1565 Bishop Pilkington granted a charter in order to boost trade. The functioning of the newly formed corporation, however, remained subject to the bishop's approval, as did the working of the new civic body of an alderman and two dozen burgesses. The charter also brought an administrative change to Framwellgate, which hitherto had had autonomous co-existence with the city, but was now united with it. In 1602 Bishop Matthew, who had been dean before his episcopal appointment, and thus had an appreciation of the city's health and workings, granted Durham another charter which gave the corporation a degree of independence. There was to be a mayor, elected by two dozen common councillors chosen from the twelve chief trade guilds, although the bishop still had power of veto.

The bishop also granted charters to individual trade guilds, which gave them a virtual monopoly of trade within the city through control of the indenturing of apprentices and certification of their competence. The religious background of guilds was played out in the festivals at the time of their particular patron saints, admission of new freemen, funerals of members or masses for the souls of departed brethren, in participation of the Corpus Christi Day procession until its suppression, and in the performance of mystery plays. In summary, their role may be seen as the medieval equivalent of the friendly societies, sick clubs and funeral clubs of later centuries.[13]

To turn away briefly from the main strand of our story, reference may be made to a particular citizen, John Duck, whom local records highlight as the city's Dick Whittington. In the mid-seventeenth century he arrived penniless in Durham, and not being member of a guild had great difficulty in obtaining work. His fortune turned when a raven dropped a gold coin at his feet. He became an apprenticed butcher, and eventually rose to become one of the wealthiest men in Durham, becoming mayor in 1680 and subsequently being made baronet by Charles II. He leased several coalmines from the Dean and Chapter, and built a big mansion in Silver Street, the most impressive multistorey timber-framed building in the city, the back of which descended towards the river. (It was demolished in the 1960s.) **(38)** He also purchased property in Haswell and endowed a hospital at Great Lumley. His memorial is for all to see in an elaborate slab tombstone in the centre aisle of St Margaret's church. **(39)**

Although civic power had been glimpsed in the charters of bishops Pilkington and Matthew, many more decades were to pass before the civil authority began to emerge effectively from subservience to Church authorities.

In 1617, on the visit of James I, the citizens of Durham presented the monarch with a petition for parliamentary representation. Although a Bill was presented to Parliament, it was vetoed on grounds that the House of Commons was already too large. However, an opportune moment presented itself when both the monarchy and bishopric were abolished during the years of the Commonwealth and Protectorate. Durham therefore achieved parliamentary representation in 1653. It was short-lived, however, ending with the restoration of the monarchy. A petition for the return of their rights was thwarted by Durham's new bishop, Cosin, who argued that he already represented the city and that a second appointment would be an unnecessary expense. At the same

Left 38 The rear of Sir John Duck's house, *c.*1960.

Below 39 Sir John Duck's memorial slab, St Margaret's church.

time the bishop rebuilt the guildhall in the Market Place, another reminder that the ecclesiastical ruler still held interest in local civic matters. Bishop Cosin, although without doubt one of Durham's great bishops, could well have the charge of autocrat laid at his door. The question remains, of course, whether he would have achieved so much, and left such a legacy for us to appreciate today, without such a strand to his character.

After seven unsuccessful attempts, enfranchisement for the city was finally achieved permanently in 1674, after Cosin's death and before the arrival of his successor. It was the last (new) borough in the country to achieve parliamentary representation. Newcastle, by comparison, had had such status since 1295. Durham had been unfortunate earlier in its timing, with dissolution and dismissal of parliaments, but opposition from bishops possessing palatinate status had been a major stumbling block. Ecclesiastical influence, however, did not disappear for several more decades. Two early MPs, for instance, were Bishop Crewe's nephew, another the son of his successor.[14] One further point is that the electorate at this time was confined to freemen, members of the city's guilds.

Apart from achieving temporary parliamentary representation during the Commonwealth, the city almost saw the founding of a university. The vacant properties of the suppressed Dean and Chapter were seen as suitable premises for such a venture by some of the gentry. Accordingly, the city's Grand Jury petitioned Cromwell in 1650 for a college to serve the north of England. Cromwell was supportive, and wrote to Parliament: 'truly it seems to me a matter of great concernment and importance, as that which (by the blessing of

God) may much conduce to the promotion of learning and piety in these poor, rude and ignorant parts'.[15]

In 1656 the Privy Council granted the petitioners' request and duly issued orders for a college to be founded in the cathedral precincts. The endowment was to be the estates formerly belonging to the Dean and Chapter. Letters Patent were issued the following year, along with details of staffing, but the project never came to fruition. Oxford and Cambridge objected to a third university, Cromwell died and the Commonwealth came to an end – and, with it, the possibility of a university.

The City Observed

From the middle of the sixteenth century accurate descriptions and the first representations of the city began to appear. Notable in this respect was Leland, the earliest of English antiquarians, who visited Durham during his country-wide survey on behalf of Henry VIII in the late 1530s.

The peninsula was conventionally recorded: 'the highest part of the hill is well walled, and hath divers fair gates', with cathedral 'very strong and fair' and castle 'standeth stately'. The building of the town he considered 'neither high nor of costely work'. His reference to the number of arches of the two medieval bridges is of interest. Framwellgate Bridge is accorded three, which may mean that the two wide elliptical arches of the replacement bridge by Bishop Langley, following the 1400 flood, were attached to a remaining smaller semicircular arch from Flambard's original structure on the landfall side of the peninsula. Elvet Bridge was accorded fourteen arches, which has been a number for subsequent debate, since some have been concealed by subsequent building at the end of the peninsula and possibly others by the build-up of ground at the lower end. The course of the river itself was a source of intrigue, given its curious loop and the narrow neck of the peninsula:

> sum hold opinion that of aunicent tyme Were ran from the place wher now Elvet Bridge is straite down by S. Nicolas now standing on a Hille: and that the other Course part for Pollicy, and part by digging of Stones for Building of the Town and Minster was made a Valley, and so the Water-Course was conveyed that way, but I approve not ful this conjecture.[16]

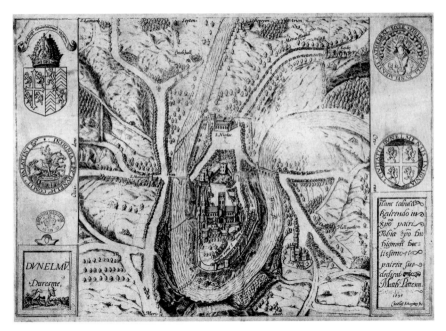

40 Plan of the City of Durham by Matthew Pattison, 1595.

The earliest stone quarries were indeed in the river gorge, both to the west and east, but if some citizens were really attributing the present circuitous course to quarrying, perhaps from stories handed down of early digging, they were clearly overestimating the ability of medieval excavation.

The first map of the city appeared in 1598, drawn by Matthew Patterson, son of a burgess, and engraved by Christopher Schwytzer of Zurich. **(40)** It is dedicated to Tobias Matthew, then newly promoted to the bishopric. The map is flanked by the coat of arms and insignia of the bishop and the seal of the city, with the Dun Cow added for good measure. The pictorial map itself is remarkably accurate, both in outline and detail, besides vividly illustrating the impact of topography on the shape of the settlement.

Soon afterwards, in 1610, John Speed produced his map of the city, an almost identical pictorial representation and equally accurate. It is interesting to view the settlement depicted on the maps with the description of the city by William Camden in his *Britannia*, published in 1586 in Latin and in 1610 in English:

Its natural site is high and strong, of no great extent, and of an oval form, environed by the river on all sides, except the north, and walled round. On the south part, almost where the river constructs itself, the cathedral rises with lofty spires and towers. In the centre is the castle, situate as it were between two stone bridges over the river on the east and west. North of the castle is the market place and St Nicholas' church, whence extends to the north a long suburb running round within the river, as also others on both sides beyond the river leading to the bridges, and having each their respective churches.[17]

The outline of the city depicted on both maps, along with Camden's description, was quaintly summarised by contemporary scholar Robert Hegg, who likened the form to that of a crab, 'supposing the city for its belly and the suburbs for its claws'.[14] The scene thus summarised, however, impressed to the extent that he immediately remarked: 'he that hath seene the situation of this Citty, hath seene the Map of Sion, and may save a Journey to the Jerusalem'. A mere two decades later Isaac Basire, a prebendary of Durham who ignored Hegg's advice and visited the Holy Land, confirmed in detail the similarity between the two cities:

> this cittie is an absolute epitome of Jerusalem, nott only for the temple or cathedral, which is a very fair one, standinge uppon the highest hill in the towne, like mount Sion, but the skirts of the towne resemble Jerusalem, and nott only that, but the country about resembles the country about Jerusalem, beinge, as scripture saith, a hilly country.[18]

The first panorama or prospect of the city appeared in the mid-1660s. It is again an accurate representation of the settlement at this time, with no obvious

41 Prospect of Durham from the south-east, by V. Bok, c.1665.

BRANCEPETH CASTLE

Brancepeth Castle is a large pseudo-Norman structure in extensive parkland standing clear of its tiny village. Its foundation predates the Norman invasion, having been erected by the Bulmer family, but the castle is primarily associated with the powerful Neville family, into which it passed when the remaining Bulmer daughter married the grandson of Gilbert de Neville, who had come across with the Conqueror. The castle was rebuilt towards the end of the fourteenth century and remained the chief stronghold of the Nevilles, who preferred it to their other base at Raby in view of its proximity of Durham.

The family was closely associated with the cathedral during late medieval times. They were generous benefactors: Ralph (d.1367) and his son, John (d.1388), with their wives, were the first laypeople allowed to be buried in the cathedral; one of their number, Robert, became Bishop of Durham (1437–57). As Earls of Westmorland they were one of the most powerful families in England (receiving mention in Shakespeare's histories) until 1569, when the castle and all property were confiscated by the Crown for the role played by Charles Neville in the Rising of the North, which was planned at Brancepeth.

During the next two centuries, when the castle changed hands several times, one interesting occurrence was the unrequited love of Mary Bellasysis for Robert Shafto of nearby Whitworth Hall, which gave rise to the song 'Bobby Shafto'.

In 1796 the castle was bought by William Russell, whose huge fortune was inherited by his son, Matthew, who had an interest in the military, was a major in the Durham militia and had a fondness for Norman architecture. These features came together in a massive rebuilding under the guidance of Edinburgh architect John Patterson, who specialised in castles. Between 1818 and 1821, therefore, the castle was rebuilt in what might be called nineteenth-century Norman. Beyond twin circular towers a huge courtyard with its buildings was enclosed by curtain walling and turrets. Billings (1846) considered it 'superior to any other battlemented edifice in the north of England'. Anthony Salvin, whose interest in military architecture was kindled while a young apprentice on the 1821 building, returned as an eminent architect in the 1860s to effect improvements inside the castle.

Brancepeth has a link with the poet Tennyson as a result of Matthew Russell marrying Elizabeth Tennyson. She was Alfred's aunt and benefactor, who supported him financially until he became established. By then the large estate was at the peak of its prosperity, but the twentieth century ushered in a changed era for all stately houses. During the First World War the castle acted as a hospital for convalescents; it then became the headquarters of the Durham Light Infantry, then a research laboratory, before being purchased in 1978 by the Dobson family, who manfully and sensitively set upon a course of restoration of their massive Grade I listed home.

sign of artistic licence. **(41)** It is sufficiently detailed, for instance, to be able to detect Cosin's new buildings on Palace Green and at the castle and St Mary-le-Bow, roofless since the collapse of its tower. More obvious is the one visible west tower of the cathedral minus its recently removed spire, also the original south face of St Oswald's church. Nearest to the observer is Hallgarth Street, diverging from Church Street and containing the prominent buildings of Elvethall Manor, originally the priory farm.

It has been suggested that the author of the prospect, known only as V. Bok, was among a small group of Dutch craftsmen and artists invited to Durham by Bishop Cosin.[16] Interestingly, it was in the Netherlands that landscape painting, with its accurate representation of scenery, first emerged in the art world. If the suggestion is correct, then the restoration bishop was not only responsible for significant buildings in the city but also for their collective recording.

EIGHTEENTH-CENTURY DURHAM

During the eighteenth century the population of the city grew steadily to over 7,500. One result was an increased density of development in the centre. Here, manufacturing, beyond that for local consumption, made a notable appearance. Most of the medieval fortifications were dismantled. The riverbanks of the meander loop, similarly relieved of its defensive function, underwent a 'greening' and became an important component of life for those at the top of society. The general appearance of the city therefore took another step nearer to that which we recognise today.

The period also saw the rise of antiquarian topographers. In County Durham the first major work was by William Hutchinson in 1787, the value of which is reflected in the extent of plagiarism among subsequent authors. His survey of the city is notable for the earliest example of the interplay between perspective and landscape experience. The section on the approach to the city repays extensive quotation:

A few paces from the south road, this English Zion makes a noble appearance. In the centre, the castle and cathedral crown a very lofty eminence, girt by the two streets called the Baileys, enclosed with the remains of the ancient walls, and skirted with hanging gardens and plantations which descend to the river Were, in this point of view exhibiting the figure of a horse-shoe ...

Approaching the city from the north, it has the most romantic and uncommon appearance: It seems to be scattered over a multitude of irregular hills ... and we discover various parts of the town, the castle, and churches, through several vallies in one point of view so that they appear like so many distinct places. The west front of the castle is seen on the summit of a ragged and steep rock, with some parts of the cathedral ... At Castle Chair, where the view is much confined, the castle and cathedral have a noble appearance: the octagon tower of the former, with the mound on

76 THE STORY OF DURHAM

42 Prospect of Durham from the north-west, by Thomas Forster and James Mynde, 1745.

which it is placed, have a grand effect. On the eminence opposite Shaw Wood, the
view just mentioned is enlarged.

Approaching from the east down the street of St Giles, we commend the second
noblest view of the city: In front, the river Were forms a fine canal through a rich
vale, crossed by Elvet Bridge, of seven wet arches, and many other land arches: the
town crowds the swift risings of the hill, pile upon pile; the castle and cathedral
church crowning the summit of the eminence.[1]

Thomas Forster and James Mynde in 1754 sketched the perspectives just
described, and although control of perspective did not begin to equal that of
Bok nearly a century before – or the contemporary Buck brothers – such licence
with realism does not negate the value. Their prospect from the north-west, for
instance, is a collage of features in which details of cathedral and castle, the
town wall, fortifications on Framwellgate Bridge, Market Place and Crossgate
are all readily detectable. **(42)**

Cathedral Living

During the eighteenth century the religious landscape changed again as the
Established Church 'settled down to a complaisant materialism'.[1] It was a
period when many leading posts within the Church were filled by sons of landed
gentry whose motive for ordination in the first instance was often the prospect
of a rich benefice – or two. Durham conformed well to this state of affairs,

for in addition to the position of dean, the posts of prebendaries were highly sought after. Boosted by the revenue of the Dean and Chapter estates, their generous stipends gave rise to the posts being widely referred to as 'Golden Canons' and their stalls 'Golden Stalls'.

It is hardly surprising therefore that hospitality and high living, rather than worship, should figure large. There was also more attention paid to the comfort of the Dean and Chapter's living quarters than to the fabric of the cathedral. By the first quarter of the century all the prebendal houses had been renovated or rebuilt, but it was not until the last quarter of the century that serious defects to both structure and fabric of the cathedral came to the fore. Before that, the main work had been repaving of the interior (mainly 1730s) and repairing of the cloisters (1760s), in which all the original tracery was replaced.

Despite an attractive lifestyle, the duties of the dean and of the prebendaries did not require them to reside permanently in Durham. In fact, some were more absent than resident in the city. A prime example is Spencer Cowper, who was dean from 1746 to 1774. He was apparently ordained reluctantly and held a prebend at Canterbury before accepting the much more lucrative post at Durham, which required official residence for only three months a year, thereby allowing him to live in the south for most of the time. He disliked the city, which appeared to him to be 'nasty and disagreeable, the streets narrow and wretchedly paved, and the houses dirty and black, as if they had no inhabitants but colliers'. Even the cathedral, with its 'massy pillars out of all proportion', failed to inspire him.[2]

In view of the priorities evident in such high living, it is little wonder that John Wesley on a visit in 1776 should remonstrate with a sermon on 'Our Lord's Lamentation over Jerusalem'. A visiting non-conformist minister, James Murray, simply remarked that 'Durham would be a very fine place, were it not for the swarms of priests'.[3]

The Cathedral and 'Improvers'

Apart from repaving the interior, no serious attention had been paid to the structure of the cathedral for perhaps two centuries. When it finally came into focus, it was largely subject to 'improvers' rather than restorers as we know them today. In 1777 Dean Rigby invited John Wooler, a surveyor and engineer from Newcastle, to compile a survey for the 'repairing and beautifying'

of the fabric.[4] Towards the end of that year Wooler presented a formidable list of defects requiring action. There was a bulge in the wall of the south aisle and a crack in the nave vaulting for much of the south side; the four corner turrets on the Chapel of Nine Altars, and gable and turrets of the north transept, were in poor condition; most window surrounds needed remedial attention; the external masonry in general was badly eroded by weathering, exacerbated by lack of downpipes to dispose of rainwater; and the north door porch needed reconstructing as the upper storey had pulled away. It was estimated that the tasks summed to eight years' work for twenty-four masons and sixteen labourers.

Work started immediately, supervised by George Nicholson. The decayed surfaces, mostly on the north face, were subjected to scraping or cutting to a depth of 2–3in, removing an estimated 1,000 tons of stone. Where such a sizeable deposit from this questionable action ended up remains a mystery. The turrets were replaced, pierced parapets were added to the two west towers and the north porch was rebuilt.

Before all the tasks recommended by Wooler were finished, a second round of repairs was sought. A new bishop (from Salisbury) and new dean (from Windsor) sought further ideas by inviting another southerner, James Wyatt from London, to draw up a plan for 'future repairs and improvements'. Wyatt, known to Bishop Barrington when he was at Salisbury, was the most fashionable architect in the country at the time and a champion of the Gothic Revival.

The list of recommendations in 1794 was again not only formidable but eventually proved to be highly contentious. Both the chapter house and Galilee chapel were to be demolished; the choir screen was to be replaced by one incorporating elements from the Neville screen and Hatfield monument; the choir extended eastwards to the east wall of the Chapel of Nine Altars to a new canopied high altar at a floor level raised to that of the existing choir; the great east window was to be replaced; a spire was to be erected on the central tower; lead on the cathedral roof was to be replaced by slates.

The Dean and Chapter were content to go along with the fashionable ideas brought to Durham from London, with William Morpeth appointed to oversee the works. Orders for the demolition of the chapter house were given in 1795, and the task was started dramatically by removing the coping stone in the vaulting. The cascading stones fell on the tomb-slabs of early bishops and priors. The Galilee chapel was next in line, and in 1796 the lead was stripped from the roof before its demolition. However, a public outcry induced the dean to backtrack, and this element, along with some other major proposals, was deleted from the schedule.

Also influential in bringing restraint was John Carter, a fierce critic of the Wyatt (Gothic) school, who had visited Durham in 1795 on behalf of the Societies of Antiquities of London and who later published criticisms in the *Gentleman's Magazine*. Two of the original recommendations, however, did proceed: the new tracery in the Chapel of Nine Altars and a new roof over the nave, where a lower pitch was feasible given that slates replaced the former heavy lead covering.

Castle

The castle was made increasingly comfortable for the bishops of the eighteenth century, even though an increasing amount of time was spent at their other palace at Bishop Auckland. An extensive adjacent deer park was considered preferable to the crowded and at times insalubrious town on the doorstep in Durham.

Externally, there were noticeable alterations to the north range, gatehouse and keep. The elevation of the north range facing the courtyard had developed a 'lean', which required a new facing. A distinguishing feature was the lattice windows topped by ogee mouldings, the characteristic feature of the Gothic Revival – or gothick, where the addition of a 'k' suggests embellishment or the theatrical. Effect, rather than function, also lay behind the creation of a more imposing gatehouse in 1791. The need for defence had long passed, but Wyatt's design resulted in a more imposing and formidable entrance, topped by battlements. The third major occurrence involved demolition: the removal of the top two storeys of the keep in 1789. Built by Bishop Hatfield, it had long been unoccupied and was becoming a danger.

Transformation of the Riverbanks

The greening of the riverbanks during the eighteenth century was a significant chapter in the evolution of Durham as we know it. The first ornamental garden on the peninsula outside the castle wall had been established by Bishop Cosin. His Bishop's Walk had been paralleled by the Prebends' Walk in the 1690s

and later by the Principal's Walk on the east side of the peninsula. During the subsequent century the Dean and Chapter, owners of most of the riverbanks surrounding the peninsula, were active landscape gardeners.

Although tree planting is linked to Dr Joseph Spence, a prebend in mid-century, trees were appearing before this time. In an era of increasing interest in topography among residents and travellers alike, the riverbanks offered innate potential. Its appreciation was guaranteed, whether the tenets for such were those of the beautiful and sublime or the romantic. A succession of refuges or vantage points presented themselves to those seeking scenic pleasure as a consequence of a peculiar arrangement of several features – a river on a sinuous course, around which paths were constructed, cascading streams and bare rock faces, springs made into features (St Cuthbert's Well, South Street Well), the Sacrist's Quarry now a wooded dell, a bridge (Prebends' Bridge) specially located to provide a visual climax to one's promenading. The south-west postern, Watergate, was enlarged at the same time to connect to the bridge.

The opportunity to provide the classic view of river, gorge, medieval mills and bridge, together with cathedral and castle, was made possible by a severe flood in 1771, which destroyed the existing bridge. The abutment of this earlier stone bridge can still be seen from the present crossing 50yds upstream into the meander loop. It had replaced a 1574 wooden crossing in 1696. The elegance of the design by George Nicholson made the new bridge itself an object of attraction, a feature reflected in the number of early paintings and prints of the view downriver with the bridge as a foreground feature. **(43)** Edward Dayes was among painters who chose this composition. Before the end of the century a host of painters had captured the view from the bridge, not least Turner, who made several sketches during his first visit.[5]

If Durham was on the circuit of painters, the poet Thomas Gray had acknowledged the attraction of the riverbanks long before in 1753:

> I have one of the most beautiful Vales in England to walk in with prospects that change every ten steps, and open up something new wherever I turn me, all rude and romantic, in short the sweetest Spot to break your neck or drown yourself in that ever was beheld.[6]

'Very beautiful' was the description given to the riverbanks by both Thomas Pennant (1776) and Sir Richard Colt Hoare (1800).[7]

43 The new Prebends' Bridge, drawn by P. Sandby, engraved by F. Chesham, 1780.

44 Prospect of Durham from the south-west, by Samuel and Nathaniel Buck, 1745.

45 Kepier: fourteenth-century gatehouse to sixteenth-century mansion. It was originally founded in the twelfth century as a hospital.

46 Crook Hall: a medieval hall adjoining a Georgian mansion.

Beauty of a more ordered kind was achieved by residents of South Bailey on the south-east slopes of the banks. Here, people of the first fortune, as they were known, extended their narrow burgage plots beyond the encircling castle wall to form a series of terraced gardens down towards the river. In places gazebos or belvederes were built on top of the wall to admire their creations. The hanging gardens at mid-century are captured in the drawing by Samuel and Nathaniel Buck. **(44)** The aerial view from the south-west, with a lowering of the near bank of the meander loop, makes visible the southern end of the peninsula. The degree and fineness of detail make it a veritable quarry of information on the city in general at this time. It also invites a point by point comparison with the description of this particular prospect by Hutchinson given earlier.

Individual gardens were also laid out by people of first fortune, particularly those in dwellings in the vicinity of the city, each interestingly located with a view of the cathedral. The earliest had been at Kepier, **(45)** Crook Hall **(46)** and Old Durham, the last-named involving elaborate terracing and by the mid-eighteenth century being a focus of concerts in the season.[8]

Durham Town

During the second half of the eighteenth century the city discarded its increasingly restrictive walls and gates. When Clayport Gate was demolished in 1791 it left only the North Gate at the head of Saddler Street. In the meantime, infilling at the rear of burgage plots and vennels had increased the density of the centre. Jettied or overhanging storeys increased the sense of overcrowding and hardly eased the health risk. In this respect the river hardly helped, since it acted as an open sewer. Passage across both medieval bridges was constricted by wooden booths or shops, some of which eventually had to be removed for reasons of safety.

The density of the central area between the two bridges clearly stood in contrast to that elsewhere and was the likely reason for contradictory opinions of the city. Thus, Celia Fiennes in 1698 had found 'the noblest, cleane and pleasant buildings, streets large well pitched', with the core described as 'a spacious place',[9] while Daniel Defoe in 1724 recorded Durham as 'a little compact, neatly contriv'd city ... well built but old'.[10] On the other hand, Tobias Smollett in *The Expedition of Humphrey Clinker* in 1771 noted that 'The streets are generally narrow, dark and unpleasant, and many of them almost impassable in consequence of their declivity.'[11] Dean Spencer Cowper, as mentioned, agreed with Smollett, and from the lofty position of the peninsula deemed Durham to be 'a rough and dirty place'.[12]

At the city's heart, the Market Place was given an enhanced focal point in 1729 when a statue of Neptune was erected on top of the new octagonal stone pant, while Cosin's guildhall was given a new classical façade in 1754. A third feature was a multi-arcaded piazza constructed in 1780 to replace the 1617 loggia, at the north end next to St Nicholas's churchyard, where stallholders contributed to the crowded business of the space.

47 Entry of Saddler Street into Market Place: Paving Commissioners' rounded corner, and timber-framed buildings with brick facing.

Efforts to control and improve the crowded conditions lay behind Durham's first two Paving Acts in 1773 and 1790. By the end of the century some highway constriction had been relieved, including that at street junctions, where buildings were trimmed back and, in places, the street-line given a rounded form. The curving entry of Saddler Street into the Market Place – formerly known as Pullein (Poultry) Corner – is a good example. The same corner also illustrates the use of brick to clad or replace timber-framed constructions. **(47)**

Brick was now the uniform material for all dwellings, the most impressive concentrations of which were in the Bailey, where several county folk had their town houses, in The College (cathedral precincts) and now also in Old Elvet. Within their dwellings a Durham tradition of elegant wooden staircases continued throughout the century. Some three-dozen remain.[13] The occupants of these houses could enjoy such diversions as concerts, card parties, general socialising – and perhaps cock-fighting for the menfolk. The first theatre in Saddler Street was established in 1722. Promenading was to hand on the surrounding riverbanks, while horse race meetings were held at Elvet. The open green on the extensive flood plain area is still known as the Race Course.

In terms of commercial enterprise, the county town developed manufactures beyond local significance. In the 1730s Mrs Clements is said to have

invented mustard by grinding mustard seed to produce a rich new condiment according to her secret recipe. The product was exported country-wide, having rapidly become popular under the patronage of George II, who, it is said, had a fondness for the lady as well as for the invention. Soon afterwards the Ainsley family became the main producers, with a shop first in Silver Street, adjoining Framwellgate Bridge, before transferring to Saddler Street. **(48)** The product gave rise to the old Durham saying: 'The City of Durham is famous for seven things: wood, water and pleasant walks, law and gospel, old maids and mustard.'

By far the most important activity was worsted and carpet manufacture. In the 1720s a mill was established in Back Lane; in the 1750s a unit in Back Lane was taken over by John Starforth on the first stretch of level ground downriver from Framwellgate Bridge on the right bank of the Wear. Towards the end of the century linen weaving was dropped from his activities so that he could concentrate on woollen cloth and carpets. It was by then a very successful venture, the largest industry in the city, with factory workers and out-workers totalling over 700.[14]

In 1796 a cotton mill was opened in Church Street, just south of St Oswald's church, by the Salvin family. It was an audacious enterprise, housed in a six-storey stone building, the stone being dug immediately to the south-west of the same extensive plot and fired by coal from the almost equally near Elvet colliery. Machinery was brought from Castle Eden. Unfortunately, however, it was completely destroyed by fire only eight years later. If the one sketch that exists of the building is an accurate depiction, then it is little wonder that pails of water brought up from the river could not save it.[15]

Durham was a strange location to choose, given the concentration of cotton to the west of the Pennines. It is believed that the Church Street textile factory was established in the expectation that Durham

48 An advertisement for Durham mustard.

would become a port, with a canal link to the sea. If so, then the strangeness is compounded, for not only is the Wear a meandering river regularly forced to flow within gorges, but three previous schemes spread over more than seventy years had already considered such a project, either to an outlet at the mouth of the Wear or by a canal northwards via the Team Valley to the Tyne – and each time rejected. It was as a result of the first such scheme that the statue of Neptune was given to the city in 1729 by George Bowes, MP for Gibside and Streatlam. Clearly none of the entrepreneurs had taken note of Celia Fiennes's assessment that the river was 'not navigable, nor possible to be made so'.[16]

Although the winning of coal from shallow pits to the south of the gorge had taken place since the second half of the seventeenth century, it was to remain insignificant until the nineteenth century when sizeable pits appeared within the city's boundary – and the county became the country's leading producer.

Josef, or Joseph, Boruwlaski (1739–1837) was a self-styled Polish count, only 3ft 3in in height, who settled in Durham after a colourful life touring the royal courts of Europe. His entrée to royal palaces stemmed from his impecunious widowed mother agreeing to him being adopted by a countess, who ensured he was taught dance and the violin by masters in Vienna and Paris respectively. They were accomplishments with which he was to become associated.

A memorable incident in Vienna was when Empress Maria Theresa sat him on her lap; when he kissed her hand, she offered him her ring, but, finding it too big, gave him one from her young daughter. Later the King of Poland gave him a small allowance, a coach for travel and royal letters of introduction. He gave concerts around Europe before coming to England, where he was presented to the future George IV, who apparently gave him not one but two watches.

After travelling around the British Isles he chose Durham for his 'retirement', being captivated by its 'romantic site' and the 'hospitality and kindness of its amiable inhabitants'. Among the latter was John Ebdon, organist at the cathedral, who lived in the South Bailey with a Greek Doric summer house on the riverside. Nearby stood his Banks Cottage, where his friend was given a home. (Since the demolition of Banks Cottage the summer house has assumed the name Count's House in popular parlance.)

For nearly four decades the Polish dwarf was fully integrated into the social scene, even if amusement was generated when he was observed in the company of his actor friend Stephen Kemble, who was a Falstaff-sized character. He published his autobiography in 1820. In a letter he once wrote a brief poem: 'Poland was my cradle, England is my nest; Durham is my quiet place where my weary bones shall rest.' His bones were, in fact, exceptionally laid to rest in the cathedral in 1837.

A full-size statue and oil painting of the count can be seen today in the town hall, together with a modest display of his personal effects, not least his violin.

six

EARLY NINETEENTH-CENTURY DURHAM

The turn of the century brought no immediate change in the evolution of the city. The opening decades may be seen as a prelude to the later dramatic economic and social change associated with the nineteenth century. Hanoverian monarchs continued to reign, with a succession of Georges giving their name to the prevailing culture. It was an age of elegance – for those who could enjoy it – before the age of industry. Markers, or precursors, of change did not appear until the third decade, with Victoria's accession and, more immediately, by reform of both parliamentary and ecclesiastical governance. We should not be surprised, therefore, that Brayley and Britton's detailed map of 1804 shows very little difference from that by Forster half a century earlier. **(49)**

Church

At the heart of the city continuity was the order of the day as the cathedral restorers carried on with works begun in the last quarter of the eighteenth century. Slating of the roof was completed, also addition of open parapets and pinnacles to provide a distinctive topping to the two western towers. The latter work actually took place during the turn of the century. In 1806 work was started on the central tower by a pupil of Wyatt. Scraping of the stonework was now discredited; instead, a covering of hard cement was recom-

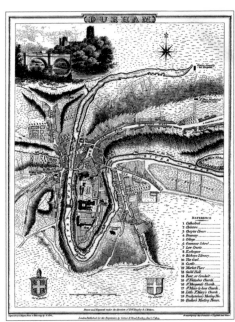

49 Brayley and Britton's map of Durham, 1804.

mended, it allegedly having the further advantage of a then fashionable 'sublime' appearance. The Chapter, however, did not concur, and the work was halted after three years. The cathedral churchyard, facing Palace Green, was levelled in 1829 and the earth banked up at the west end to assume its present form.

Inside the building the appearance was to remain largely unaltered until later in the century. The stonework continued to be refreshed with a lime covering, as it had been since the initial Puritan action. Such action was not without its critics. Witness the attack on the practice by archaeologist Sir Robert Colt Hoare following his visit in 1800; he was no friend of Wyatt's methods of restoration in general:

> Repairs if they are necessary should certainly be done but not in the manner they are here done. In entering these grand Gothic structures the mind should be impressed with religious awe suited to the place. Here no such effect, no such sensation, no fine mellow tints on the columns, no effects of light and shade, no relief to the eye – one general glare; and one general yellow wash has been unmercifully smeared over the walls, ceiling and every part of this reverend building. Even the marble monuments have not been spared.[1]

One event unconnected with restoration was the opening of the tomb of St Cuthbert in 1827. It was motivated by the desire to test a persistent rumour among some that a substitute body had been inserted in the sixteenth-century turmoil, a rumour recently broadcast in Sir Walter Scott's 'Marmion':

> His reliques are in secret laid;
> But none may know the place,
> Save of his holiest servants three,
> Deep sworn to solemn secrecy,
> Who share that wondrous grace.[2]

Accordingly, the large Frosterley marble covering in the feretory was raised, and search revealed three coffins, with the bottom one containing the body of St Cuthbert. His skeleton was in a series of fine wrappings, with a pectoral cross on his chest. Alongside was a separate skull (that of St Oswald), possessions of the saint and gifts by King Athelstan in 934. Durham's saint was re-interred and the treasures carefully preserved. The tomb of Bede was also inspected in 1830; afterwards an inscription was made on its simple covering.

Georgian Durham also saw the continuation of the Prince Palatinate, with its eminence and special privileges, and a Dean and Chapter known for its golden stalls and plurality of livings, along with part-time residency. At one point the dean and three of the prebends also held bishoprics. This centuries-old pattern, however, came to an end following reports by the Ecclesiastical Commissioners in 1835 and 1836, hard on the heels of the Reform Bill. As a result, the bishop was deprived of the status of prince-bishop and his income was greatly reduced. The Chapter was reduced to a dean and six canons, who were to receive a fixed salary and not revenue from its estates.

Durham's last prince-bishop, William Van Mildert, **(50)** a distinguished scholar, had been appointed in 1828. The following year there was what was to prove the last festal banquet in the grand manner of the long tradition of his predecessors in the episcopal palace. The occasion was the visit of the Duke of Wellington and Sir Walter Scott, who were entertained along with one hundred guests, many of them nobility. Sir Walter Scott later recorded that it was 'as splendid and striking a fete as I ever witnessed'. Apparently 189 bottles of wine were consumed, which must have contributed to the enjoyment of the evening.[3]

With talk of reform in the air, and with the notion, emanating from the Archbishop of Canterbury himself, of using Church revenues to make voluntary acts of endowment, both bishop and Chapter anticipated the likely outcome of the Church Commissioners' ecclesiastical reforms by deciding that a positive outcome would be to divert some of the Church's wealth towards the founding of a university. Durham, after all, had been a seat of learning from the beginning, had founded Durham College in Oxford and had been about to receive university status in the seventeenth century when Cromwell's death brought a sudden end to the project. Confidential talks were therefore held among key persons, including the Archbishop of Canterbury, secrecy being maintained in order to thwart other possible contenders. In June 1831 Canon Charles Thorp wrote tentatively to Bishop Van Mildert:

50 Bishop William Van Mildert, last prince-bishop of Durham, 1826–36.

I would fain bring before you the project of a university to be attached to our College. A slight extensions to the establishments and a few Professorships founded by the body in the Cathedral would effect the object. It would give to the Dean and Chapter strength and character and usefulness – preserve the revenues of the Church to the North – and prevent the establishment of a very doubtful academic institution which is now taking place in Newcastle. I trust you will not think me a projector beyond what the times require.[4]

Although Canon Thorp is now generally credited with being the first to raise the idea of a university, there remains the enigma of a reference in the *Quarterly Review* in 1829 by the poet Robert Southey to the munificence of a lady waiting for the establishment of the northern university.[5]

The bishop was in full agreement, and progress was rapid. In September the Chapter unanimously approved the idea, and the two archbishops and Prime Minister were informed. Parliamentary approval quickly followed, and royal ascent was given in July 1832. Durham was finally a university city.

Town

The town in the shadow of the peninsula exhibited greater affinity with the preceding eighteenth century than with that which was to emerge in the first part of Victoria's reign. In the Market Place, the medieval church of St Nicholas, with its tower, still acted as long-stop, with the arcaded piazza of 1780 against its churchyard. Westwards was the large townhouse, known as New Place, but dating from the time it was the townhouse of the Earls of Westmorland (the Nevilles), from whom it was taken in 1569 for participating in the Rising of the North. Next to it stood the guildhall, rebuilt by Cosin in the seventeenth century, although given a classical façade in 1754. Overall, Neptune, atop of the pant, stood watch. **(51)**

With expansion of trade, restriction of movement became an increasing problem. For this reason Clayport, the exit from the Market Place to Claypath, had been demolished in 1791. In 1803–04 Elvet Bridge was doubled in width by extending on the upriver side, and the booths that had colonised the bridge were removed. In 1818 North Gate, at the top of Saddler Street and the last and most impressive of the medieval defensive gateways, was demolished. **(52)** Its removal had to await provision of a new prison, for part of Bishop Langley's

51 Market Place, 1820s.

structure had acted as the city's gaol, along with a 'House of Correction' beneath the upper end of Elvet Bridge.

When North Gate was demolished, the buildings adjoining were set back in order to widen the street and were re-fronted. At the corner of Saddler Street and Owengate a subscription library and newsroom was erected in 1820; four years later a mechanics' institute was erected in the same street. With a theatre already nearby, Saddler Street, connecting the peninsula with the Market Place, was clearly established as the city's social axis.

The new prison, at the head of Old Elvet, is of interest in that it saw the introduction to Durham of architect Ignatius Bonomi, who was to have a distinguished career for forty years working from his office in the city.[6] He arrived in 1813, after two other architects had severally mishandled the project for a new county, or assize, court and prison first begun in 1809. The court is fronted by large Tuscan columns beneath a giant portico; **(53)** behind, and out of sight, Bonomi built three separate wings for males, females and debtors.

The area in which the court was located had long been popularly known as 'Popish Durham', so it was appropriate that the first Catholic church to be built in the city since the relaxation of the anti-Catholic laws (in 1796) should be built here. St Cuthbert's (1826) was again Bonomi's work, on this occasion applying a Perpendicular Gothic style. His versatility in style is illustrated in a third structure at this time, for the so-called Count's House on the riverbank,

exhibiting a Greek Revival appearance, has been attributed to Bonomi. The structure was actually a summer house for a nearby house where Polish dwarf Count Boruwlaski lived.

If we turn from details of architecture to social townscape, a general lack of progress is evident. An Act of Parliament set up a board of Durham Paving Commissioners, which was to be in charge not only of paving but also cleaning, draining, lighting and policing. Some improvement was achieved in paving, but especially in lighting, so that comfort of movement about the town became less dependent on the weather and time of day.

The Commissioners appointed contractors to be responsible for lighting the town. Some 180 lamps, powered by whale oil, were erected and lit from sunset to dawn. The quality of illumination provided might be judged from the fact that lighting was deemed unnecessary at the time of full moon. Disruption – not helped by vandalism – caused the Commissioners to take over responsibility from the contractors for closer control, but soon another source of power arrived that offered to increase the illumination four-fold.

In 1823 a gasworks had been erected at Framwellgate Waterside, on the left bank of the Wear, and a contractor immediately offered to light the town for the same cost as oil. It was accepted, and by the last days of December of that year gas pipes had been laid and all the gas lamps lit. A few areas lay beyond the network, and here oil lighting continued, but for the town as a whole its reception can be gauged from the comment of the *Durham County Advertiser*:

> The change which this substitution of gas for oil has effected is perfectly surprising, for we behold a city, long notorious for its nocturnal darkness, becoming at once, perhaps the very best – at all events one of the best – lighted towns in the kingdom ... Thus Durham has exchanged a light, barely sufficient to render 'darkness visible', for one of great beauty and brilliancy.[7]

The success of lighting notwithstanding, living conditions in pre-Victorian Durham

52 North Gate, Saddler Street.

Ushaw College is a nineteenth-century creation, a Catholic seminary for the north of England situated in an elevated position 4 miles west of the city. It was founded in 1808 by refugees from the confiscated English college at Douai in France, where for two centuries students had been educated and trained when Catholics in this country were denied such. It grew into an imposing collection of buildings which, after an initial large Georgian block, became an essay in Gothic Revival led initially by Augustus Pugin, England's leading architect, designer and artist. After his death in 1852 his ideas were continued by two sons, notably Edward (E.W.), and even by his grandson. Other notable architects were Joseph and Charles Hansom, the former being the inventor of the hansom cab. The environment produced was a synthesis of devotion and austerity.

Among the clustered array of buildings the most notable are the college chapel, library and refectory. The first, dedicated to St Cuthbert, was originally built by Augustus Pugin in 1848, but such was the college growth that it was doubled in size by Dunn and Hanson in 1884. Careful dismantling enabled many of the original fitments and much of the original glass to be retained. The refectory was also by Pugin, including the massive tables and benches. The library (J. and C. Hansom) contained some forty works that belonged to the pre-Reformation monastic collection at Durham. Among its many relics was a gold ring taken from Cuthbert's coffin in 1540.

An increase in Catholic ordinands, and the addition of a junior school, brought extensive building throughout the nineteenth century, including five more chapels, dormitories, swimming pool and gymnasium. (The chapel of St Michael's, by E.W. Pugin, is listed Grade I.) Outside, stone walls were erected for unusual games of keep-up and trap brought from Douai. Nearby was a large farm complex designed by Joseph Hansom.

At its peak the college was home to over 400, but with the rapid decline in vocations for the Roman Catholic Church in the last half-century the seminary, which had produced five Cardinal Archbishops of Westminster, closed in 2011. A charitable trust has been set up, and it will possibly become a centre for Catholic scholarship and heritage.

remained little changed, with a marked contrast between the peninsula and the remainder of the town. One simple indicator of the contrast was the distribution of households valued at £10 or more a year, which figure was taken as the threshold for franchise eligibility in the 1832 Reform Act. On the peninsula practically 100 per cent of the houses qualified (three-quarters also had resident servants), in St Nicholas's and St Oswald's parishes the figure dropped to just over half, in St Giles's parish it fell below two-fifths.

53 The Assize Courts, Old Elvet.

For the town as a whole there were still no sewers or drainage system; rather, evil-smelling sewer ditches and public garbage heaps. Conditions underfoot were not helped by horse droppings, aggravated on market days by the slaughtering of stock and poultry in Fleshergate and Pullein Corner. Few houses had a water supply. The steadily increased density of the central area, aggravated by such conditions, resulted in the city having the highest death rate in the county. It was to take two government reports in the 1840s into the sanitary condition of Durham, and the powers of the Commissioners to be taken over by the Corporation, before the old gave way to the new.

The new era was also to be one of political reform. Its beginning was marked by the Great Reform Bill of 1832, which brought to an end some 180 years of Durham's history during which time the city's two MPs had been elected solely by freemen. A residential qualification was introduced, which for freemen meant living within 7 miles of the city. A fifth were thereby excluded. More significantly, certainly in the long term, was the fact that for the first time franchise was given to householders. Properties valued at £10 or more a year meant that some 800 householders were given the vote. This compared with some 420 resident freemen and another 550 within 7 miles. Comparatively few were doubly qualified.[8]

Residential qualification for the city – and the fact that the county was at long last given parliamentary representation – meant that delimitation of a parliamentary boundary was necessary for the first time. The boundary, by making use of natural features where possible, was more generously drawn, especially to the

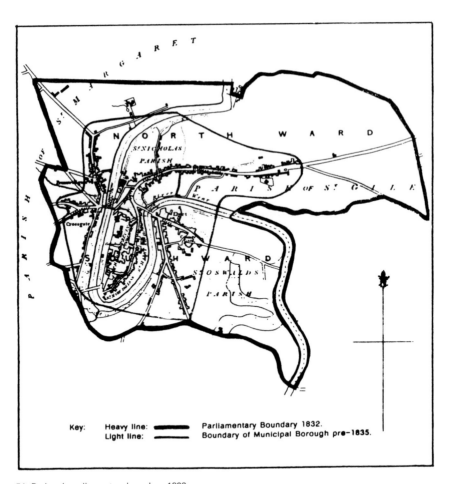

Key: Heavy line: ▬▬▬ Parliamentary Boundary 1832.
Light line: ▬▬▬ Boundary of Municipal Borough pre-1835.

54 Durham's parliamentary boundary, 1832.

east, than that of the existing, more schematic boundary of the borough, **(54)**
although it included little more population. Soon afterwards the same boundary
was taken as the most appropriate division for the local government unit when
municipal government was reorganised in the Municipal Corporation Act of
1835. The latter boundary remained unaltered for the rest of the century.

Reforms notwithstanding, on the eve of Victorian England continuity rather
than change still characterised the city. Thus the authoritative survey by histo-
rian Robert Surtees could conclude, if somewhat poetically, that:

> Few places, perhaps, of equal extent and antiquity have fluctuated less than Durham
> in wealth, population, or other circumstances. The new cathedral has replaced the
> prior and convent ... The Wear yet flows (dark as is its downward course) unpolluted,
> if unenriched, by the neighbouring mines, and the same quiet atmosphere still invests
> the ancient irregular City, founded in the bosom of woods and hills and water.[9]

seven

VICTORIAN DURHAM

Victorian Durham participated only modestly in the unprecedented population growth and feverish industrial expansion of the nineteenth century. Population census figures summarise the justification for such a statement, for while the county's total increased tenfold during the century the city's figure little more than doubled. In terms of settlement totals, the city in 1801 had only recently conceded first place in the county to Sunderland, but by the end of the century, although its population had reached 16,000, it had slipped to twelfth position. Industrial-urban growth along the river estuaries of the Tyne and Tees across the county boundary put its regional ranking in even poorer light.

The lack of any large-scale industrial activity may be attributed to an absence of level sites with access to water transport, together with late and circuitous connections to the rail network as a result of topographical and land-ownership difficulties. Thus, while many Victorian cities grew dramatically as a result of focusing on a single industry, Durham continued to evolve as a multifunctional settlement, albeit that several of its activities and roles were relatively modest.

A Railway Town

Although County Durham saw the birth of railways, the single most potent symbol of vitality in Victorian England, it was almost half a century later before the county town was to achieve direct access to London. The city even possessed three railway stations, but none provided the impetus for commercial growth. Perhaps growth would have been encouraged by the level terrain beyond the head of Old Elvet had the Sunderland and Durham Railway not encountered ecclesiastical opposition in the 1830s to its wishes for a terminal

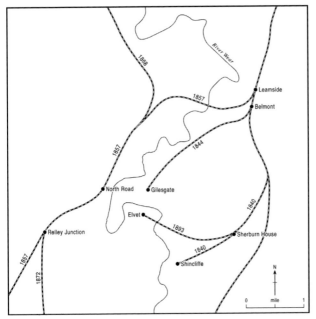

55 Arrival of the railway.

at Elvet. Instead, the line from Sherburn House had to terminate at Shincliffe village 1½ miles south-east of Durham.

A line was eventually brought in, but not until 1893 following a City Council petition to the directors of the North Eastern Railway, **(55)** but by then opportunities had been exploited and patterns set, such that it was surely difficult to conceive where sufficient potential traffic, passenger or goods, was to be generated.[1]

The city's first station was that at Gilesgate, beyond the top of Claypath, in 1844. It was the terminus of a branch line from Belmont ('Durham Junction') of the Newcastle and Durham Junction company. Strangely, the arrival of the iron horse in town received no comment from the local *Durham Advertiser*. The station building itself was of stone in an elegant Georgian style by J.T. Andrews. The main route from York to Newcastle had bypassed Durham to the east; Belmont, 2½ miles to the north-east, was the nearest point to the city. George Hudson, known as the 'Railway King', had largely pioneered the east coast route, so that it is instructive to note his comment in the *Advertiser* on the difficulties he encountered with the major landowners:

It is always unpleasant to come into contact with so influential and so important a body. The Dean and Chapter professed to be willing to meet this company on liberal terms, but he could not but say that the professions they made and the conduct that they subsequently exhibited were perfectly irreconcilable.[2]

The whole line became known as the North Eastern Railway in 1854 as a result of an amalgamation of companies.

The city's North Road station opened in 1857. Northward, its rail joined the main line at Leamside, just a mile from Belmont, which it superseded. It required an impressive viaduct over the Wear gorge downriver from Kepier. Southwards, the line went as far as Bishop Auckland, beginning with an even more impressive viaduct. The station itself was a dignified, if modest, construction in stone designed by T. Prosser in Tudoresque style, complete with arches and battlements.

Although only on a branch line within County Durham, the celebration of its opening contrasted markedly with that thirteen years earlier at Gilesgate. Realisation of the prosperity that railways could bring – and had brought to other towns – was doubtless a key factor. Moreover, the station was both prominently sited, unlike Gilesgate's which was half-hidden, and alongside a spectacular curving viaduct of eleven arches. The latter was Durham's contribution to an age noted for its towering monuments, and was by far the biggest piece of construction in the city since the Norman cathedral. On 1 April 1857 crowds gathered at the decorated station and adjacent slopes to greet the first train, which was carrying NER directors and guests from Leamside. Its arrival was met by the mayor and a salute of cannon. The train then pulled out over the viaduct to a salvo of artillery from the grounds of Mr John Lloyd Wharton of Dryburn Hall. Having reached Bishop Auckland, they soon returned, to

56 Railway viaduct under construction, 1856.

57 Embankment for the viaduct under construction, 1855.

be greeted this time by the Durham City Band and a champagne luncheon in the town hall.

The advent of the railway in general and the viaduct in particular markedly changed the appearance of the edge of the western rim of the bowl in which the city lies. The viaduct represented a massive engineering feat, achieved by NER's own engineers, Richard Cail and Thomas Harrison. The wide opening into Flass Vale, the source of the Mill Burn, was alternately marsh or peat bog, such that tree trunks had to be sunk up to 50ft depth to give stability to the 100ft high pillars. **(56)** The total span of some 280yds would have been more but for an embankment built out into the Vale of sand and clay excavated from a 90ft cutting at Redhills, **(57)** part of the north-south ridge that had been the site of the Battle of Neville's Cross. For rail travellers journeying north, the effect of the cutting was to produce a suddenness in the appearance of the spectacular scene of cathedral and castle, surely the most famous carriage window view in England. John Ruskin, who declared the view from just above the station one of the wonders of the world, was among the early visitors to appreciate the newly provided vantage point. It is said Queen Victoria would order her train to slow to take full advantage of the view while crossing the viaduct.

Durham eventually assumed its rightful place on the main line between London and Scotland when its North Road station was linked directly north by a line from Newcastle along the Team Valley to Newton Hall in 1868, followed in 1872 by a southern line laid from just beyond the Neville's Cross ridge at Relly Junction to link with the early main line route at Tursdale.

Coal Mining

Although the Victorian city found itself in the middle of the evolving Durham coalfield, the county town did not become a coal capital. Early patterns of exploitation had already been established in the north and north-east of the county, along the incised valleys of the lower Wear and Tyne, to which wooden wagonways further channelled exports of so-called 'sea coal'. Several of the exporting centres then became rail foci, which in turn encouraged the assembly of materials and the emergence of secondary industries. Differential fortunes, however, were not always appreciated by many elsewhere, who perceived the nineteenth-century city and county as one. A good example is the admission of Matthew Arnold who, on his travels from the south in 1861, had to admit to surprise at what he saw: 'the view of the cathedral and castle together is superb; even Oxford has no view to compare with it ... I was most agreeably disappointed, for I had fancied Durham rising out of a cinder bed'.[3]

While Durham did not become a centre of coal mining, it was nevertheless surrounded by mining activity as dozens of shafts were sunk and colliery branch lines criss-crossed the area. **(58)** The peak of activity in the vicinity of the city was in the 1860s and 1870s as the focus of nineteenth-century mining in the county moved slowly from west to east, having begun on the exposed part of the field and been worked increasingly towards the coast, with the eastward-dipping seams requiring ever deeper shafts.

Geological conditions within the eastward-dipping seams varied, such that the number

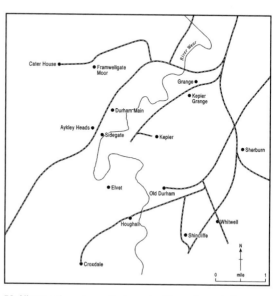

58 Nineteenth-century collieries and colliery railways in the vicinity of Durham.

and thickness of coal seams was the outcome of conditions during deposition and on subsequent geological history. In the Durham area, for instance, of the five workable seams only three were present to the east of the city. Thus, while the Hutton seam was widely extracted in the area, the pattern of working of the lower Busty seam stopped abruptly east of the city. **(59, 60)** Both maps well illustrate the extensive nature of extraction, being the collective underground work of the many collieries shown in the earlier map. The boundaries of colliery leases are clearly decipherable.

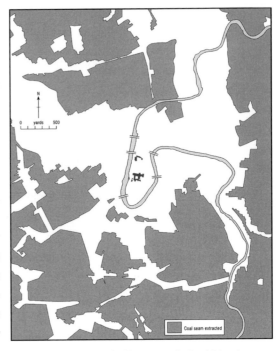

59 Coal extraction from the Hutton seam in the vicinity of Durham.

A more local variation underlies the lack of exploitation beneath the peninsula, where, even if the authorities had given permission for working, efforts would have been thwarted. Here, during a glacial period, the Wear was aligned to a much lower sea-level and consequently deeply incised its bed, well below the present. Despite subsequent infilling in post-glacial times, the buried river bed presented insurmountable drainage problems to any would-be extraction. Thus, the river gorge, which played a key role in the defence of the early city against Vikings and the Scots, performed a much later protective role in warding off an underground attack.

The era of shaft mining in the city, as opposed to shallow bell pits, began in 1828 with the sinking of Elvet colliery. **(61)** Most of the larger pits followed a decade or more later, with Framwellgate Moor (opened 1841) and Old Durham (1849) the two biggest. Both were worked by the Marchioness of Londonderry, the first leased and the second owned, and were the only two pits to have coke ovens attached. They also had by far the largest number of tied cottages, more than 180 at Framwellgate Moor and 250 on Gilesgate Moor in a compact series of streets called New Durham.[4]

By mid-century almost 700 mineworkers were living in the city, barely one-tenth of whom had been born in Durham. The bulk were immigrants from elsewhere in the North East, with the remainder from other mining districts, as well as some Irish immigrants. During the second half of the century the number of mineworkers doubled – during periods of full employment, that is. A pit such as Elvet colliery, which produced only household coal and was therefore limited to a single market, could also vary in employment seasonally between summer and winter, depending on demand.

Above ground, apart from the appearance of spoil heaps and, of course, branch railways, the mining industry brought about an extension of Durham's suburbs beyond the rim of the central bowl for the first time. Eastwards, associated particularly with the Old Durham and Kepier collieries, rows of miners' cottages grew along the Sunderland Road east of the ancient village of Gilesgate. Northwards, equivalent housing was erected along the road leading to Newcastle.

The only reported instances of subsidence attributed to mining related to Elvet colliery. In the 1830s St Oswald's church had to be virtually rebuilt. Intriguingly, colliery plans show no workings beneath the church, while Bonomi, the architect engaged to repair the building, referred to 'shrinkage of subsoil' and 'creep'.[5] Whatever the reason, the chancel, south aisle, part of the north

wall and clerestory were rebuilt, and the roof lowered. Immediately after the turn of the century subsidence as far away as the city's workhouse at the top of Crossgate, well over half a mile away, was incontrovertibly linked to the colliery. Pillars of coal that should have been left to support the overhead strata had been taken during back-working of the seam.[6] The colliery owner was sued, the company went into liquidation and the mine was abandoned.

One central role that the county town did perform was to host what became known as the Durham Miners' Gala. In August 1871, only two years after the founding of the Durham Miners' Association, there

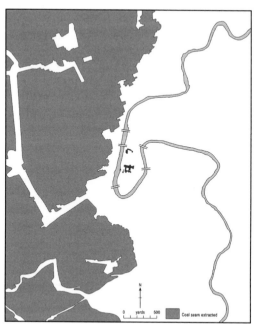

60 Coal extraction from the Busty seam in the vicinity of Durham.

61 View north-east towards Elvet colliery, c.1900.

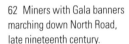

62 Miners with Gala banners marching down North Road, late nineteenth century.

was a gathering of Union Lodges from across the county in Wharton Park. With attendance variously estimated between 3,000 and 5,000, and with speeches, brass bands and sports, it was the first 'Big Meeting'.[7]

The following year, when the attendance jumped to 20,000, the event was held on the Race Course, on the way to which bands marched past a welcoming party of VIPs on the balcony of the Royal County Hotel. The city's magistrates, perhaps understandably, granted licences somewhat reluctantly for the refreshment in booths for the gathering on the Race Course, but, having done so, tradition for the largest trade union meeting in the country had been set. Leading members of the Labour movement were a feature from the beginning; in 1882 the radical Russian prince Propotkin addressed the gathering. In 1897 the final element, signifying full acceptance, was the addition to the programme of a service in the cathedral. Thus did the Miners' Gala echo the Corpus Christi celebrations of the medieval Trade Guilds, which processed to the cathedral and ended with mystery plays in the Market Place. **(62)**

An Industrial Town

With one or perhaps two notable exceptions, the manufacturing industries of Victorian Durham were those that might have been found in any town of comparable size – small-scale, serving the local market and of a kind that could have been present in the previous century. Such activities were flour-milling, hide-tanning, paper-making, rope-making and hat-making, for example. A leather works in a four-storey building on Framwellgate Waterside and iron foundries amid nineteenth-century artisan housing in Crossgate and Atherton Street may have been more significant, but the overall list was hardly impressive. It certainly did not impress the correspondent of *The Builder* who visited the city in 1866:

> Durham was never fitted by position or shape to be a great emporium of trade, and the railways which of late years opened up other towns and cities and gave them a great manufacturing stimulus, but little disturbed the slow progressive trade of this ancient city ... The making and consumption of beer seem to be the best trade, – nearly a hundred public and beer houses attest the fact.[8]

Although not a large operation, mustard-making had a reputation well beyond the city. There were three power-driven mills producing ground mustard in Victorian Durham with outlets in Silver Street, Saddler Street (later transferred to Waddington Street just beyond the railway viaduct) and Gilesgate. The first was the best known, being the inheritor of the secret recipe of Ainsley's mustard invented by Mrs Clements in the previous century. The pride and jealousy with which the recipe was still guarded is evident from contemporary advertisements. **(63)** Guarded, that is, until 1904, when both recipe and factory were sold to Colman's of Norwich.

An event that was eventually to have more than local significance was the arrival in Durham in 1872 of two brothers from Rochdale, Thomas and James Harrison. **(64b)** Occupying a former paper mill in Hawthorn Terrace, their organ-making

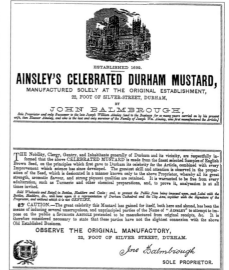

63 An advertisement for Durham mustard.

64 Prominent Victorians: (a) William Henderson, (b) James Harrison, (c) Revd John Bacchus Dykes.

enterprise, though small, quickly established a wide reputation, which from the turn of the century was to spread worldwide. The reason for their choice of Durham is unknown; within the city, and in a street off Hawthorn Terrace, there was already another small organ works. The general timing coincided with an era of church building and the increasing installation of organs.

The one industry that can be said to conform to the stereotypical image of Victorian enterprise is that of carpet manufacture.[9] It had a long antecedence, with cloth weaving having been present in the city for several hundred years and, most recently, with the large carpet factory of John Starforth, which had closed through bankruptcy in 1805. One person who had clerical experience working in Starforth's factory was Gilbert Henderson, who in 1813 transferred his own small operation from the village of Kirk Merrington to Durham, along with the nucleus of a workforce. Vacant premises were leased to the rear of the town hall and in Back Lane. In 1824 his wife assumed charge until their two sons, John and William came of age, by which time there were 150 working in their premises and many more employed in their own homes.

The Back Lane area, once studded with ramshackle buildings, became lined with modern factory units, (65) including a workroom and showroom designed by W. Hodgson Fowler, a distinguished architect who succeeded Sir George Gilbert Scott as architect to the Dean and Chapter. Different sections of the works undertook the whole process, from treating raw wool to the finished product. Steam-powered looms were introduced early, patents acquired, a design artist appointed, even its own fire brigade formed. The company had a London office and showrooms, which was important for its national and international customers, for by mid-century Hendersons was concentrating on the upper range of the market. An article by a correspondent in the *Mercantile Age* was one long paean of praise. The Durham Axminster, it reported, 'bears the most favourable comparison with the costliest fabrications of Turkey', while its 'world-famed' Brussels carpet was only one of several desirous specialities and novelties.[10] The company exhibited at the Great Exhibition of 1851 and subsequently won many awards at international exhibitions in Paris, Vienna, Dublin, New York and Philadelphia.

The workforce, which had grown to 600 by 1860, had its own library, concerts and talks, and an annual outing to the seaside for workers and their families. On these occasions William Henderson and his wife would greet the gathering assembly in the Market Place to the accompaniment of a band before making their way to the station. On their return they were led by the band back down North Road to Silver Street and the Fleece Inn. What happened then is not reported.

In the best tradition of Victorian industrial entrepreneurs, the two brothers both widened their business interests and became influential in local civic affairs. John, who became chair of the board of directors of the Consett Iron Company (when it was one of the biggest such operations in the world), had been one of the first councillors chosen for the St Nicholas ward after the Municipal Corporation Act of 1835, and became MP for the city in 1864. He lived in a classical stone villa built on the Claypath spine looking towards the castle and cathedral. William **(64a)** became mayor of the city in 1849, and was deeply involved in the building of the new town hall and covered market in the 1860s.

By the mid-1870s the two brothers were in poor health, and eventually John's youngest son, Arthur, assumed control for the remainder of the century. Durham carpets maintained their worldwide reputation, with North American

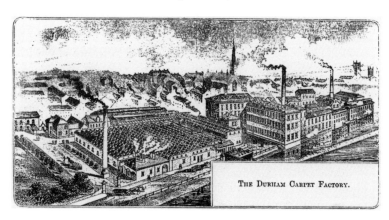

65 Hendersons'
Carpet Factory
c.1880.

THE DURHAM CARPET FACTORY.

and Australian markets strengthening previous ties, thereby ensuring that the name of Durham evoked more than a famous cathedral.

Another person deserving of acknowledgement for his influence in the town, although hardly in terms of employment, is the previously mentioned Ignatius Bonomi. Of Italian origin, he arrived in 1813 and practised in the city for forty-seven years from offices successively in the North Bailey, Old Elvet and his own house, Elvet Hill. One of his apprentices was John L. Pearson, who subsequently designed Truro Cathedral. Apart from half a dozen buildings in the city, he was for twelve years architect to the cathedral (where he carried out restoration of the Nine Altars, inside and out, and parts of the south face) and County Bridge Surveyor (designing Shincliffe Bridge, also the Stockton to Darlington Railway bridge over the Skerne, which is portrayed in John Dobbin's well-known painting).[11]

Market Town

The hub of any market town is of course its marketplace, which in Durham had been the civic focus ever since Bishop Flambard's clearance of early settlement from the peninsula and creation of the Bishop's Borough. It was a relatively small space that could easily become congested. Early in the present century the piazza in front of St Nicholas's church was demolished, much of the churchyard removed and even the east end of the church itself shortened by removing the chancel in an effort to make more space for stalls and carts. **(66)** Quarterly horse fairs certainly did not ease the situation, particularly the March fair, which lasted three days. The fairs remained a feature until late in the century, when they were transferred to Old Elvet. These events obviously brought business to the centre, although complaints of unruly evening behaviour appeared regularly in the local press.[12] On the other hand, complaints were also made against rowdy behaviour by university undergraduates,[13] who again brought increased trade to the town.

The face of the Market Place changed dramatically after the mid-century. The north-west frontage at the time was the guildhall, with its mid-eighteenth-century classical façade, and New Place, variously a public house, workhouse and tenements. The latter building had long lost its attractiveness, while the guildhall, and the mayor's chamber behind, were now both certainly too small for conducting business. The driving force for change was carpet entrepreneur and mayor William Henderson, who was also the most generous of nearly 300 subscribers. The building he envisaged had to be 'an edifice in the best style of ancient architecture, yet having a proper regard to their modern notions of comfort'.[14]

P.C. Hardwick of London was duly engaged for a 'new public hall and piazza'. The 'best style' proved to be Perpendicular Tudor, both for the new façade of the guildhall and for the main hall, the latter being modelled on Westminster Hall, complete with hammerbeam roof. A large stained-glass west window incorporated historical characters

66 North end of Durham Market Place, c.1850. St Nicholas's church, a Norman foundation, had been shortened in 1841 before demolition in 1857.

and scenes, not least the guilds' Corpus Christi procession. At the same time a 'new' or 'indoor' market was constructed (in 1852), partly beneath the town hall and continuing down the slope towards the river to end in a stone wall, which echoed the former city defences.

At the north end of the Market Place St Nicholas's church, a Norman foundation, was replaced by a neo-gothic structure with a spire rising 160ft, the first such in Durham. The architect was J.F. Pritchett of Darlington (1858), and was rated at the time by the *Illustrated London News* as 'the most beautiful specimen of church architecture in the north of England'.[15] In 1861 a large statue of the third Marquess of Londonderry was placed in relation to the new buildings and immediately provided a strong focal point for the whole Market Place. The work by R. Monti from Milan was an early example of electroplating.

In the totally renewed north end of the Market Place the pant, topped by the statue of Neptune, now appeared somewhat shabby, and for a brief while this much older feature was under threat. In 1863, however, Neptune was positioned atop a redesigned pant, following public support in letters to the local press – including one by 'Neptune' himself. Later in the century the opposite end of the Market Place received uplift and dignity, led by three banks that emphasised the financial function of the space – National Provincial (1876), Barclays (1887) and Lloyds (1900).

Shops lining the streets leading from the Market Place were at their most distinctive and exuberant by the end of the century, not least when decked out for festivals. **(67)** Circulation in the Market Place and in the centre's narrow streets remained a crucial factor for the city's livelihood, **(68)** a factor emphasised in the necessary repair and widening of Framwellgate Bridge. It was the only river crossing between the centre and the railway station, and was already congested and unlawfully narrow at the Silver Street end. Now it was about to have to take the additional traffic diverted by the NER to its North Road station from its Gilesgate terminus. When the Town Commissioners were reluctant to act, the City Corporation took charge, and appointed Bonomi to undertake the necessary work in 1856.

The street from the bridge to the station, North Road, had only been opened in 1840, but in time became lined with several prominent buildings – the Bethel chapel (1853) and miners' hall (1875), with St Godric's church nearby. Beyond the viaduct was the County Hospital (1853) and St Cuthbert's Anglican church (1863). It constituted the new, direct route out of the city to Newcastle. Framwellgate, the old route to Newcastle and formerly a wealthy merchant colony, had by now declined in social status. **(69)** Elsewhere, most notably in the vicinity of the viaduct, a dozen or more streets of artisan terraces had sprung up, uniformly built of red factory brick with roofs of Welsh slate.

Above 67 T. Brown & Son, Silver Street, game and poultry shop, *c.*1880.

Right 68 Congestion in the Market Place, *c.*1880.

69 Framwellgate Peth, looking towards Millburngate, *c.*1900.

Above Framwellgate, and immediately above the station, William Wharton of Dryburn House had created a park on a knoll overlooking the heart of the city. In an evocation of the picturesque, a mock gun battery was erected to pin-point for guests the exact spot from which best to experience the visual climax. Appreciation became widely shared when the park – Wharton Park – was given to the city in 1915.

A University Town

The young university added to the roles which the town played. It gave rise to new buildings, initially on the peninsula, brought colour to its streets and slowly boosted the sport of rowing. The Victorian institution, however, never fulfilled the expectation of its founders. The reason lies in a combination of factors: increasing ease of travel with the spread of railways; the lack of significant ben-efactors (there was no government funding); and the shadow of the Dean and Chapter, initially in terms of governance and long-term in the perception of the institution as one for theological students. Thus the number of undergraduates, which rose to 130 in the 1840s, had dropped to less than half of this by the early 1860s, such that closure was contemplated. After a Royal Commission in 1862 numbers rose to 200 by the 1880s and remained stable until the end of the century, by which time the first women undergraduates had been admitted.

Despite its slow growth, the university left its mark in the material fabric of the city core, and was associated with some notable personages and innova-

70 Cosin's Library, 1842. A university examination is in progress.

71 The university observatory.

tions. In terms of fabric, the castle keep was rebuilt for student accommodation (1840), replacing the earliest residences in Cosin's Hall, a lecture room was provided on the site of the bishop's coach-house and stable (1841), followed by Hatfield Hall (1846) and a library (1858). Initially Bishop Cosin's library had been used, both for reading – Bishop Van Mildert had added a gallery around the room to house books for students – and for examinations. **(70)** All the new buildings were designed by Anthony Salvin, consultant architect to the cathedral and a County Durham man who had been a pupil at the grammar school when it was on Palace Green. (He designed the new school when it was transferred across the river to Quarry Heads Lane in 1844.) One further piece by Salvin was the university observatory (1840), a classical stone building with a dome, which was the first university building south of the river. **(71)** The land had been given to the institution in 1832 by the ecclesiastical authorities, who gifted further extensive parcels in 1846 and 1851. The observatory is notable today for having the UK's longest unbroken sequence of weather recordings from an undisturbed location.

Hatfield Hall, the university's second hall and named after the benefactor bishop of Durham College, Oxford, catered for 'persons of very limited resources'. In practice, this meant that, unlike University College – and all Oxbridge colleges – all undergraduate rooms were let furnished and all meals were taken in common. It subsequently became the pattern countrywide.

The young university attempted other, academic, innovations, being the first to establish a school for civil engineering and pioneering astronomy, but such ventures eventually failed. Newcastle was the more obvious location for scientific study, and in 1879 the warden, William Lake, founded a School of Science across the Tyne. Failure in Durham, however, could not be laid at the door of two academic giants, the Revd Temple Chevallier and James Finlay Weir Johnston. The former was professor of mathematics combined with astronomy, reader in Hebrew and divinity, and university registrar. Outside the university he was vicar of Esh, a village 3 miles west of the city. James Johnston was reader in chemistry and mineralogy and a founder-member of the British Association for the Advancement of Science. His benefaction also led to the establishment of the city's Technical School.

The student body was also not without its characters, most noticeably one of its earliest students, Edward Bradley (1845–8). He was ordained after graduation, but was more widely known as an artist/cartoonist and author who contributed to several periodicals, including *Punch* and the *London Illustrated News*, often writing under the pseudonym Cuthbert Bede. His best known work, *The Adventures of Mr Verdant Green, an Oxford Freshman* (1853), has many illustrations that may be recognised as Durham, although on his publisher's insistence the story is set in Oxford. It was a 'book for the rail', became a best-seller and was followed by two sequels. All three tell of undergraduate pranks

72 & 73 Edward Bradley, 'Ye Freshmonne: His Adventures at Univ. Coll. Durham', Part 1 *(left)* and Part 2 *(right)*.

played on the gullible Verdant Green. The novels even circulated in the USA, sometimes with the subtitle 'The Dude'. Bradley left several etchings of student life in Durham and their privileged quarters, but his sequence of eighteen sketches, entitled 'Ye Freshmonne: His Adventures at Univ. Coll. Durham', **(72, 73)** expresses more humorously that there was more to student life in Durham than academic study.

It is perhaps noteworthy for a future clergyman that none of Bradley's sketches depicted attendance at services in the cathedral. They were compulsory for all students, once on weekdays and twice on Sunday. Morning prayer was held in the Chapel of Nine Altars until the 1870s, when it was transferred to the Galilee chapel. Here, initial complaints about the cold were replaced by those about sulphurous fumes. Relief was achieved when human discomfort was reinforced by signs of disintegration of the Purbeck marble columns, caused by the introduction of coke braziers. The episode is still recorded in the stonework.

The County Town

Ecclesiastical dominance over both town and county had long eased, and during the nineteenth century political reform and social change resulted in enlarged or new activities in the county town. This occurred despite its population being far outstripped by several towns elsewhere in the county, which were boosted by industrial growth. Perhaps a slower growth led to a more healthy environment. Certainly, the correspondent of *The Builder*, referring to sanitary conditions, remarked that the city had 'few of those barbarous lanes that disfigure, and which are a disgrace to, such towns as Newcastle and Sunderland. Although the streets are narrow, they are kept pretty clean.'[16]

Durham's advantage lay in its historical momentum, a location in the middle of the county astride the Great North Road and, now also, the main line railway. Its cathedral was unchallenged, of course, and directly from it had sprung the North East's – indeed, North's – first university. Unsurprisingly, the city was the chosen location when the church created the first teacher training colleges for men (St Bede's, 1839) and for women (St Hild's, 1858).

The county hospital (1859) was naturally in Durham, as were the county court and gaol, with an annual procession to the assize court in Elvet during the visit of judges, who were lodged in the castle. The new police headquarters

74 The new shire hall, Old Elvet, *c.*1905.

75 Unveiling of Lord Londonderry statue, 1861: a contemporary painting.

(1880), a strong brick statement of Victorian gothic, was appropriately adjacent to the court. The strongest statement of all, however, was the shire hall (1898), designed by H. Barnes and F.E. Coates, for the newly formed County Council. Situated in Old Elvet, its fiery red self-cleansing brickwork with copper dome is unlike any other building in Durham. **(74)** Inside, on the walls and ceilings, are highly glazed decorated tiles, best described as 'High Victorian Railway', while staircases are of white Sicilian and dark Frosterley marble. The whole composition is what contemporaries termed 'a magnificent pile', but from the point of view of both scale and configuration it overwhelmed the elegant Georgian street in which it was planted.

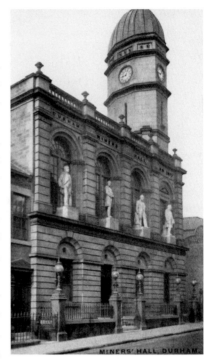

76 Durham Miners' Hall, North Road.

In 1861 the county town was considered the appropriate location for a commemorative statue of Lord Londonderry. The third Marquis of Londonderry (1775–1854) had a distinguished career as a soldier and ambassador before marrying Frances Anne Vane-Tempest, heiress to extensive property and coal mines in the east of the county. The marquis took control of his wife's estates, sank deep shafts and built railways to export coal from Seaham Harbour, a port-settlement entirely of his creation, and Sunderland. The placing of the statue in the city was therefore to honour achievements elsewhere. In this respect it is noticeable that the sculptor, Raffaelle Monti, put him in hussar's uniform on a charger, noticeable also that the picture of the unveiling shows four army corps present. **(75)** His downtrodden workforce of miners were therefore spared the sight of a sculpted coalmaster on their annual visits to the county town for the Big Meeting, which began in the next decade.[16]

The county town, the venue for the miners' annual Gala, was the obvious choice for the union's headquarters. Accordingly, a neo-classical stone building was opened in North Road in 1875. **(76)** From street level, more noticeable than the building's copper-domed octagonal clocktower, were the life-size sculptures of four pioneers of the Durham Miners' Association standing upright on pedestals on the front elevation.

The city was also the venue for social events or gatherings in addition to that of the miners. Outdoor activities included horse-racing, cricket and rowing. The most notable event was the annual rowing regatta, first held in 1834, some years before the Henley Regatta was inaugurated, when a hitherto annual mixture of racing and merriment to celebrate the victory at Waterloo was put on a proper footing. The nerve centre was the Boathouse, situated on the right bank just above Elvet Bridge. **(77)**

Throughout the nineteenth century the owners of the Boathouse, besides constructing pleasure craft, specialised in the design and building of racing craft. The most significant occupant was John Hawkes Clasper, who moved from Tyneside to Durham in the early 1860s. **(78)** He was a notable boatbuilder and oarsman, who invented and patented the fin keel and improved the sliding seat invented by his father.

John brought with him the aura of the remarkable Clasper family. His father Harry had designed the first keel-less rowing boat, the prototype for all modern racing craft, as well as several other key innovations. As an oarsman he was a legend in his lifetime, with special rail excursions to see him in action. Musical hall songs were also composed about his exploits. He was world sculling champion and, with four brothers, defeated the Thames Watermen, considered undisputed world champions, in a challenge match on the Thames. He rowed regularly in the Durham Regatta from 1841 and with John, his eldest son, from the mid-1850s. Durham therefore merits mention in the annals of rowing history.[18]

One particular sporting event that merits mention is a cricket match held on the Race Course in 1849 between 'Eleven of All England and Twenty-two of

Left 77 The Boathouse, *c.*1860.

Below 78 An advertisement for John H. Clasper, a Durham boat business, 1863.

DURHAM.

JOHN H. CLASPER,
BOAT BUILDER,

Begs to inform Rowing Clubs and the Aquatic public generally, that after ten years' practical experience with his Father, H. CLASPER, the inventor of the present Outrigger, he has commenced business on his own account at Durham; and having secured very commodious premises, he has every facility for building, on the shortest notice, Racing or Pleasure Boats of the most approved model, for combining speed with durability.

TERMS FORWARDED ON APPLICATION.

J. H. C. IS OPEN TO TRAIN GENTLEMEN FOR PRIVATE OR OTHER MATCHES.

N.B.—Boats let out on hire, and a stock of Nets and Second-hand Boats constantly on hand for Sale.

the Durham Club'. It was reported in both *The Times* and the *Illustrated London News*. The latter also included an engraving of the scene from Pelaw Wood, **(79)** the artist of which was almost certainly Edward Bradley, the previously mentioned Durham graduate. The match was won by All England by forty runs or 'notches'. This was considered a good performance by Durham, since the visiting team included some cricketing giants of the day. In their next match the England XI beat a Scottish XXII by 161 runs.

One periodic macabre event in the county town that ceased after 1865 was the gathering to witness public hangings on the green in front of the Court House in Old Elvet. Thus the cast-iron balcony of no. 30 opposite could no longer offer an advantageous viewpoint of this gruesome spectacle.

Cathedral City

The cathedral, whose role in the city had been widened by its close link with the university, continued to generate employment, both directly and indirectly, beyond its ecclesiastical function. (Although the diocese of Newcastle was created in 1882 out of the ancient diocese of Durham, it had no obvious effect on the city.) Two deans, George Waddington and William Lake, were in office for most of the Victorian era: both were wardens of the university and both were notable for the extent of cathedral reordering, or 'improvements', which they spearheaded. By the end of the century the interior of the building had essentially assumed the appearance we see today.

Dean Waddington (in office 1840–69) was responsible for insertion of stained glass in the rose window, and brought about a significant reordering through the engagement of the architect, Anthony Salvin. The major project undertaken in the 1840s sought to expose the view of the whole length of the cathedral. To this end, the Langley chantry tomb in the Galilee was moved in order to open the great west door and the seventeenth-century carved oak choir screen, surmounted by the organ, was dismantled. The woodwork around the feretory was also removed, and for good measure the wooden screens and doors to the north and south of the choir were also dismantled. Even Cosin's font was moved. The result was disappointing: if anything, the building's impressiveness appeared diminished. The former sense of enclosure, from within the choir, can be gauged from the painting by Edmund Hastings, 'Cathedral Choir, Assize Sunday, 1835', showing both choristers and dignitaries at the annual service. **(80)** Salvin also replaced the pulpit with a stone version and reinserted round-headed Norman windows in the north and south aisles of the nave, removing the medieval tracery in order to re-create the original form.

In 1859 George Gilbert Scott was brought in to repair the central tower. The unsatisfactory Atkinson cement was removed, buttresses restored, stat-ues renewed or replaced and the top finished off with pierced battlements and pinnacles. The distinguished architect had wanted to cap the tower with an open crown or corona, similar to the one on St Nicholas's in Newcastle, which he was later to restore.

Scott returned to initiate a huge restoration programme in 1870, a year after the appointment of Dean Lake (1869–94). Thirty years had elapsed since the extended view of the interior of the cathedral from west to east had been opened. The long vista, with walls covered in unrelieved whitewash and light entering through plain-glass windows, was no nearer gaining general

80 'Cathedral Choir, Assize Sunday, 1835' by Edmund Hastings.

approval. Consequently the whitewash was removed from the body of the church to reveal the warm sandstone, and stained glass was inserted in the south aisle and Chapel of Nine Altars. The Langley tomb was replaced, Salvin's pulpit was replaced by an ornate marble one, a pelican lectern was introduced and the floor of the choir and sanctuary was repaved with coloured marble. Cosin's wooden choir stalls were also restored. The critical reinstatement, however, was the new choir screen, a project that drew considerable controversy.

Scott's screen, signifying a division of space without visual blockage, was a delicate triple-arched marble structure. Dean Lake favoured the design, but Bishop Baring, at the opposite end of the spectrum of churchmanship, was opposed. Their two widely differing views on the project were voiced in both the local and national press. The service to mark the reopening of the cathedral on completion of the restorations in 1876 was attended by almost all the clergy in the diocese; the bishop was among the few absentees. The *Durham County Advertiser* was diplomatic in its view of the new screen: 'To say that it is in keeping with the Norman nave would be saying too much; to say that it is a fine work of art would be saying too little.'[19] The Durham and Northumberland Archaeological and Architectural Society was less respectful in its response to both screen and the accompanying alterations, and 'hoped that by the next century the whole of these so-called improvements would be swept away'.[20]

The last major happening was the rebuilding in the 1890s of the chapter house by Charles Hodgson Fowler, close to the original design. The work was undertaken as a memorial to Bishop Joseph Barber Lightfoot (1879–89), a much loved and distinguished scholar-bishop. In its obituary *The Times* wrote that his learning was 'as solid and comprehensive as could be found anywhere in Europe'.

One other cathedral person who had an impact beyond Durham was John Bacchus Dykes, who was precentor from 1849 to 1862, before crossing the river to become vicar of St Oswald's until his death in 1876. **(64c)** Dykes composed over 300 hymn tunes, no fewer than a tenth of which were included in *Hymns Ancient and Modern*. Many of the tunes are named after local scenes. Perhaps the best known is the tune 'Hollingside' to 'Jesu, lover of my soul', which derives from his vicarage in Hollingside Lane.

THE DURHAM LIGHT INFANTRY

The county's own regiment, the Durham Light Infantry, was formed in 1881, but its genesis was in 1758 when John Lambton, of Lambton Castle, raised the 68th Regiment of Foot as a new unit in the British Army. They fought with Wellington and in the Crimean War before merging with the 106th Regiment of Foot and with the county militia and rifle volunteers. (Each county had its militia, which consisted of local gentry as officers, with part-time soldiers initially chosen by ballot. Their role was home defence, allowing the professional army to fight abroad.) The headquarters of the new regiment was briefly in Sunderland before transferring to Newcastle.

Despite its name, a minority of men actually came from County Durham. This situation was not reversed until the mass of volunteers from the county's farms, mines and shipyards during the First World War. In 1914 the regiment had nine battalions; by 1918 the figure had risen to forty-three, of which twenty-two saw active service. The DLI took part in every major battle of the First World War and shared in the heavy loss of life – some 13,000 – and casualties. Six of their number won the Victoria Cross.

During the Second World War, when over 3,000 sacrificed their lives, eleven battalions fought at Dunkirk, North Africa, Italy and Germany, besides Burma. Two Victoria Crosses were won. After the war battalions were engaged in Korea, Cyprus and Borneo.

In 1968 the Durham Light Infantry was merged with three other county regiments to form The Light Infantry. The Colours were paraded for the last time in Durham Cathedral in December 1968. Its headquarters had earlier been transferred to Shrewsbury, having been at Brancepeth from 1939. There was a further merger in 2007, when the new regiment was renamed The Rifles.

In the same year that the regiment lost its county appellation, a permanent memorial was opened in the city. At Aykley Heads a DLI Museum and Art Gallery, designed by J.O. Tarren and P.M. Caller, houses a wide range of historical mementoes and records, from military vehicles to the first VC of the Second World War, won by Richard Annan.

eight

DURHAM IN DEPRESSION

I f Durham's growth during the Victorian era was less than spectacular, certainly in comparison to most neighbouring towns, then in the first half of the twentieth century the city did little more than mark time. The most obvious measurement, that of population, needs interpretation since the boundary was twice moved outwards, in 1905 and 1955.[1] The first expansion added 180 acres along the western boundary, the second, 3,000 acres to the south, north and west. If totals are calculated for the 1905 boundary area, the city grew by barely 1,000 souls in the first two decades of the century; if the 1935 boundary area is used, the interwar years actually saw a decline in the total population of the city, which had only just regained its 1921 figure of 19,000 by 1951.

Durham, both city and county, shared in the suffering of the First World War to the extent that approaching one-third of some 40,000 men serving in the Durham Light Infantry lost their lives. Following cessation of hostilities, the city was disadvantaged in economic terms by being the capital of a county more severely hit by depression than most other areas in the country. Its vitality as a service centre for the area around suffered accordingly for a long period. Mining employment in the city area was declining, and coal extraction had passed its peak before the turn of the century as the industry moved progressively eastward. Its manufacturing had received a severe setback when its biggest unit, the carpet factory, closed in 1903, while throughout the period its university remained small and at times appeared near to closure.

Mining Industry

Several of the smaller pits within, or in the vicinity of, the city had closed early in the last century, while the larger operations of Houghall and Old Durham

had closed towards the end of the Victorian period. Elvet closed at the turn of the century, as previously mentioned, following a court case brought because of subsidence it caused. Durham Main was closed in 1920, Framwellgate Moor a decade later. The very last working was at the Aykley Heads pit, which was revived in a small way between 1934 and 1949.

The county as a whole, however, continued to be one of the country's major coalfields throughout the first half of the twentieth century, a factor that naturally impinged on the county town. A new, more impressive miners' headquarters was erected at Redhills, just to the north of the railway. **(81)** Designed by H.T. Graydon, and completed in 1915, it is the city's prime Edwardian structure – and the miners' response to the County Authority's new shire hall. In fact, within four years the miners had also taken over the shire hall, for, when in the 1919 county elections Durham became the first authority in the country to return a socialist majority, the obvious chairman was their own leader, Peter Lee. He was later to become president of the Miners' Federation of Great Britain; and in 1947 a government new town in the east of the county was named after him. The union also built a residence in the city for their leader.

The city was also the venue for the miners' annual Big Meeting, which reached its peak in this period. Every second Saturday in July Durham was taken over by miners and their families, who could number 200,000 – ten times the population of the city. The most vulnerable shop windows had to

81 New Durham Miners' Hall, Redhills, 1915.

be boarded up, such was the pressure of bodies in Durham's narrow streets. Well over a hundred colourful banners were carried aloft, ahead of each colliery band, followed by its workforce and their families. With the salute in front of the Royal County Hotel, dancing in the streets and speeches, picnics and all the fun of the fair on the Race Course, the event was appropriately likened to a living Breugel.

Merriment evident at the Gala could hardly have been a pervading characteristic for the rest of the mining year. The industry was dangerous and poorly rewarded; lock-outs by coal-owners and strikes brought untold hardship. For three years in the 1920s union funds were so depleted helping unemployed miners that there was nothing left to organise a Big Meeting. Depression did not begin to lift until the mid-1930s, by which time the workforce had been reduced by two-fifths.

The Second World War also caused the Gala to be suspended. Its resumption in 1946 was a historic occasion, for the Labour Party had just won an overwhelming majority in the national election and had immediately nationalised the mining industry, although vesting day was to be 1 January 1947. The leader of the Labour Party, traditionally the first speaker at the Gala, was therefore the Prime Minister, Clement Attlee. He was not alone, for according to the local

82 Prime Minister Clement Attlee and the Rt Hon. Herbert Morrison on the balcony of the Royal County Hotel acknowledging Gala crowds, 1949.

newspaper 'it seemed as though the whole government had been evacuated for the weekend from Whitehall to Durham'. The American Ambassador to Britain also attended. In the euphoria surrounding the day Nye Bevin, claiming he had always hated coal owners, assigned the past to history by remarking: 'This Gala marks the end of a black era and the beginning of a brighter one. Young miners need never fear unemployment again or suffer victimisation at the hands of vicious colliery owners.'[2]

The day finished with a celebratory dinner in Durham Castle. The portraits on the walls of the great hall, which had witnessed many grand occasions in the past, must have been surprised at the new order.

The Gala continued to attract huge crowds for the rest of the 1940s, with some estimates putting the figure at a quarter of a million. Certainly, while the Labour Party was in power, the Prime Minister and various cabinet members continued to attend the Big Meeting. **(82)**

Manufacturing Industry

The last of the small trades (tallow chandlers, paper-making, glove-making) became extinct in the late nineteenth century, and the well-known Ainsley's mustard works and printing works closed in 1904, but the most significant loss came with the sudden closure of Henderson's carpet factory. After three generations, and with business interests developed elsewhere, Henderson's were persuaded to sell when approached by Crossley of Bradford. The reason for the purchase became clear immediately, namely to eliminate an important competitor. Plant was removed, and rights to colouring, designs and trademarks obtained, as well as a network of contacts.

Within months of the closure, however, a phoenix began to rise from among the empty and silent sheds. Hugh Mackay, **(83a)** who had worked in the Henderson plant from the age of twelve and risen to works manager, bravely leased some of the buildings and machinery and began to produce relatively low quality but popular carpet squares. Slowly, using the expertise still present, the new venture began to make its own high-quality patented carpets –Yakcam (Mackay spelt backwards), Durmac (from D<u>ur</u>ham and <u>Mac</u>kay) and Lani (derivation unknown).

Throughout the interwar period, despite the depression aggravating what tended to be a seasonal activity, numbers grew slowly. In 1924 Laurence

Mackay took over the concern on the death of his father; in 1930 the leases on all of Henderson's factory units were purchased. By this time there were showrooms in five cities and the Durham workforce numbered 150. Despite its undoubted success, this figure is only half the number formerly employed by Henderson. Part of the explanation lay in greater mechanical efficiency.

For the last decade of the period under review the factory marked time. Carpet-making ceased in 1940, when the machinery was adapted for the manufacture of blankets, webbing and camouflaged nets for the war effort. For the years immediately after the war the rationing of raw materials until 1950 precluded any further advance.

The second activity for which Durham was known, that of specialist manufacture of organs, achieved a national reputation during this period. Thomas Harrison's two sons, Harry and Arthur, had taken over in 1894. Between 1904 and 1939 they built or rebuilt no fewer than nineteen cathedral organs, as well as those in Westminster Abbey, King's College Cambridge and the Royal Albert Hall. Success was achieved with a staff complement that never exceeded sixty.

The Peninsula

Attention on the peninsula for the first half of the twentieth century was not focused on the cathedral but on the university and, in particular, the castle. The university itself remained a small institution, which contracted further during each of the two wars. The 200 students of 1900 was fewer than in the late Victorian era, and had only risen to 400 by 1939. In 1932 the centenary of its foundation passed without celebration, officially postponed through lack of funds, an echo of the reason for cancellation of the miners' Big Meeting a few years ear-

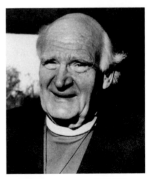

83 Prominent persons: (a) Hugh Mackay, (b) Dean Alington, (c) Lord Ramsey, (d) Thomas Sharp.

lier. In this instance repairs to, indeed, the saving of, the castle required more than all the funds at the university's disposal.

The castle's problems derived from the Norman decision to place the structure on the strategic neck of the peninsula, which was subsequently discovered to be the only section where solid rock was not immediately below the surface. Here, some 40–70ft of unconsolidated sands, clays and broken freestone rested on top of the rock. Further, a lack of any substantial footings or foundations meant that settlement or movement had gone on unhindered for almost 1,000 years.

In 1901 the south wall into the courtyard, which had previously been 'shaved' and resurfaced, was tied to the north wall across the Norman Gallery by three rows of steel rods. However, when an inspection revealed serious defects a national appeal for £30,000 was launched. The *Graphic* (11 July 1925) had a picture across its centre pages with the caption 'Durham Castle: A Magnificent Pile Threatened with Destruction.' In 1928 it was discovered that the south wall had increased its lean into the courtyard to 2½ft, having pulled the north wall. The great hall had developed several cracks, and its west wall was leaning on the edge of the drop to the river.

The original appeal total was clearly insufficient, thus an urgent national appeal was launched in 1928 for £150,000, equivalent to several millions in today's terms. **(84)** Flag days were held locally; the Lord Mayor of London opened a Mansion House fund; in the House of Lords Durham's bishop, Hensley Henson, inquired about government assistance, but was informed that there were no powers to contribute to preservation or maintenance of a building that was inhabited. The ironic, if not absurd, situation evident in the last response was accurately summed up in the *Durham University Journal*: 'While the Castle stands the Government can do nothing, but if a large portion of it should slide into the river, as it probably will before long, then it can take over what is left and preserve it as an historic ruin.'[3] The *Durham County Advertiser* actually published a sketch showing how a ruinous castle might appear.

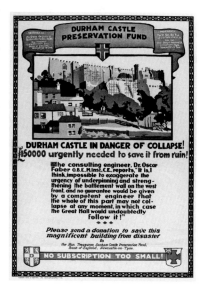

84 Durham Castle appeal poster, 1928.

The appeal had come at an unpropitious time, and funds were nearing exhaustion when the Pilgrim Trust stepped in with a generous donation in 1935. A further donation in 1937 allowed the work to be completed by the end of the decade. The massive operation involved drilling tunnels beneath the building, inserting steel ties to massive concrete blocks buried in the courtyard and the injection of thousands of tons of concrete to form a solid foundation The massive operation in progress closely resembled that depicted on the appeal poster. **(85)**

The most significant academic interwar occurrence for the university was a new beginning in science in 1924, with the opening of the Dawson Building, named after the County Director of Education. It was the university's first foray since the observatory south of the river. Located on South Road, this part of the university's extensive estate, acquired between 1832 and 1851, was to become known as the Science Site.

In 1945, when the new Labour government sought to expand tertiary education, Durham's vice-chancellor, Sir James Duff, took the opportunity to argue for a larger, collegiate institution, one that was better balanced than the current one, about which there hung 'a certain air of spiritual mildew'.[4] A blueprint for growth was drawn up accordingly, although it was not realised until after the turn of the half-century. The first two of the hill colleges, so-called because of their position on rising ground of Durham's rim south of the river, were St Mary's (a hostel for women from 1899 and recognised as a college in 1919), where a foundation stone was laid by Princess Elizabeth in 1947, and Grey College, which received approval in the same year. By 1950 the student population was just over 1,000.

The cathedral in the first fifty years of the twentieth century was more noteworthy for its personnel than for any major alterations to its structure. At the beginning of the period Dean Kitchen was noted for banning students from the cathedral following unruly behaviour. In the interwar years Bishop Hensley Henson is remembered for his apparent lack of sympathy with miners' actions, arguing against the use of strikes as a bargaining tool and being against their campaign for a minimum wage. He also warned against charity 'rotting the character'. Such was the miners' antipathy that during the 1925 Gala the dean, mistaken for the bishop, had to be rescued by the police. Fortunately, a happier relationship existed with Dean Cyril Alington **(83b)** (1933–51), who installed a miners' memorial in the cathedral in 1947. It incorporates part of Cosin's former choir screen.

Early during Dean Alington's time, the precious wall paintings in the Galilee chapel were revealed. More precisely, it was the painted scenes on the wall above the north arcade that were exposed for the first time, since there are suggestions that the paintings of bishop and king behind the altar of Our Lady were already known. Exposure came when the covering of limewash was removed in the mid-1930s. It is fortunate that the limewash removal of the 1870s in the main body of the church did not extend to the chapel. Techniques had now advanced – certainly beyond that of caustic soda and wire brush of the Victorians.

Dean Alington also put the Choristers' School on its present footing, founded the Friends of the Cathedral and showed equal concern for the city in spearheading the formation of its civic amenity body, Durham Preservation Trust (now City of Durham Trust). He also took the initiative in the acquisition of a property in the Bailey for a community centre, now known as Alington House, in recognition not only of his part but equally the role of his wife's activity within the centre. He was also a notable hymn-writer, besides being a prolific writer of poems, novels and religious works.

Another person who loved Durham – and who in turn was loved by its citizens – was Michael Ramsey.[5] **(83c)** He arrived in 1940 as canon-professor in

85 Durham Castle undergoing restoration, 1929.

theology and later became Bishop of Durham before becoming Archbishop of York and subsequently the distinguished one-hundredth Archbishop of Canterbury. On retirement he returned to Durham once more and played a full part in the life of the cathedral and university. A further feature was his daily constitutional down the Bailey to Prebends' Bridge and back.

Town and Townscape

Since the city contained no dynamic economic activities to compensate for the depressed county, it is little wonder that the appearance of the county town should begin to reflect that of the surrounding region. Photographs of the time depict the dilapidation or unattractiveness of some areas. **(86, 87)** At the same time it remained a small town largely provisioned by local agriculture, a world we have now lost. It was still possible, for instance, to see sheep herded through central streets to the local abattoir in the 1930s. **(88)**

The area of greatest dilapidation was the Millburngate-Framwellgate area, which underwent slum clearance during the 1930s, with the population rehoused over the rim of the bowl east of Gilesgate and at Sherburn Road. No fewer than 600 new houses were erected; there were two visits by royalty. **(89)** The untidy derelict space by the riverside remained undeveloped for a further three decades. It was presumably Framwellgate that so shocked Joan Conquest, a novelist visiting from London. She wrote to the local newspaper: 'Within the shadow of your glorious cathedral men, women and children are living as the law would not allow us to keep the meanest pig. I have never seen anything like it.' [6]

Perhaps the one bright spot for many was the entertainment brought by the spread of moving pictures. The first theatrograph had appeared in 1896 in the People's Palace in Court Lane. In subsequent years, when it was an itinerant business, moving pictures were shown in the assembly rooms in the North Bailey, the drill hall in Gilesgate, occasionally in the town hall and even at the annual spring fair on the Sands and at the Miners' Gala in July. The first cinema was the Palace Theatre (1909), formed by converting part of Henderson's carpet warehouse. Cinemas then followed in North Road (first in the old Miners' Hall, then the Essoldo, 1934), and Claypath (Palladium, 1929), and nearer to newer housing at Gilesgate Moor (Crescent, 1928) and Sherburn Road (Majestic, 1938). [7]

86 View east over Framwellgate-Millburngate, c. 1930

87 Looking to lower Crossgate, with spire of St Nicholas in the distance, c. 1925.

A different kind of fun palace came in 1942 when an ice rink was built just downriver from Framwellgate Bridge. If the idea was that of a local man, 'Icy' Smith, the stimulus was the number of Canadian forces stationed in the area. Initially an open rink, it was soon given a canvas cover, before being roofed over in 1947 in utilitarian fashion and illuminated by a neon sign at its gable end. One interesting feature was that river water, diverted by the medieval weir past the remains of the Bishop's Mill, drove a hydro-electric turbine, the output of which was used to produce the ice.

The most comprehensive survey of the condition of the city was undertaken by Thomas Sharp, **(83d)** who brought to bear both a sympathetic and pro-fessional eye. He was born in Bishop Auckland, in the centre of the county's south-west coalfield, then a scene of dereliction. He wrote several books in the

88　Sheep being driven up Crossgate, past St Margaret's church, *c.*1938.

1930s, introducing the concept of 'townscape'; became reader in town planning at Newcastle (part of Durham University); was president of both the Town Planning Institute and Institute of Landscape Architects; and compiled a series of development plans for several cities, including Durham, in the 1940s. The city received some earlier attention in his essay in the widely circulated *Britain and the Beast* in 1937.[8] Although in comparison to the county the city was said to stand out 'like a flower among filth', he made clear that the epithet refers solely to the peninsula.

A comprehensive survey of the stagnation that the city had undergone during the interwar period, if not for longer, is given in Sharp's *Plan for Durham*, compiled while he was consultant to the city and published in 1945.[9] The following extensive quotations summarise the existing state:

> Besides its individual features of grave and commanding beauty, the city has extensive (and unfortunately, prominent) areas that are mean and depressing: and it has a general squalor and untidiness which is as inescapable as the beauty itself. The river that runs so romantically through its tree-bowered gorge is as black as ink and seems to have the consistency of treacle. The whole place is dirty and shabby and dilapidated.

89   King George VI and Queen Elizabeth visiting new housing on the Sherburn Road estate.

The number of dilapidated and of actually derelict shops is quite considerable. In Claypath, especially, there are a number of shops which are actually tumbling in; and others are empty and about to do so. In Saddler Street there are also one or two which are empty and dilapidated beyond hope. But many in the North Road also, seem to maintain only a very tenuous existence. Even in Silver Street and the Market Place there are shops which look anything but flourishing. Indeed, everywhere the quality of the shops is poor and drab.

There is probably no town in the country with a more difficult traffic problem than exists here ... [A]n almost intolerable pitch of congestion had been reached nearly a decade ago.[10]

It is interesting to note that it was reaction to such widespread depressing conditions that led to the creation of the city's Preservation Society: its founding aim was to protect the city's buildings, not from the threat of inappropriate development, but from loss through neglect and deterioration.

Sharp's outline development plan reflected his disapproval of suburban sprawl and low-density residential development, together with the aim of maintaining a tight distinction between town and country. And, like all documents,

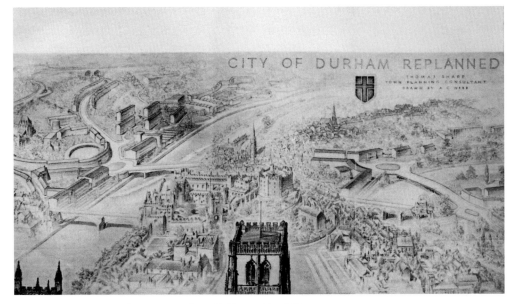

90 Artist's impression of Durham as envisaged in Thomas Sharp's Plan.

91 Police box in the Market Place.

it was a child of its time. Witness, for instance, the statement that 'a civil aerodrome will almost certainly be required'.[11] Different functions were grouped about the centre: a new shire hall was the focus of his new road descending the south side of the Claypath spur; a new town hall, bus station and technical college were to be beyond the Claypath underpass across the river at Framwellgate; an 'ensemble' of library, museum, theatre and baths lined Elvet Waterside behind Old Elvet; university colleges were to line the slopes of Pelaw Leazes to adjoin the colleges of St Hild and St Bede. **(90)**

Traffic circulation was recognised as essential to the success of any plan. The narrowness of the central arteries had been recognised by the first Paving Commissioners. More recently the local newspaper had echoed a universal opinion in its editorial in 1927, with its comment that 'Some other way of entering and passing out the central part of the City must be found in order to bring Durham back into the importance it once occupied in the business and commercial life of the County.'[12]

The Pant had been dismantled in 1923 (and Neptune re-sited in Wharton Park). A police box was introduced in 1932, later aided by traffic lights on the two bridges and, later still, a television monitor in the police control box. **(91)** However, traffic relief rather than control was required, for, as Sharp pointed out, fifteen roads funnelled into three narrow streets to meet in the Market Place. Sharp had proposed an internal bypass or through road in the mid-1930s, but was opposed by the County Authority, which had its own scheme. The latter did not have a spur breaking out of lower Gilesgate to relieve Claypath of through traffic, and neither, therefore, a Claypath underpass. Instead, it was proposed that the road from a new Elvet bridge would circle round while rising on a 25ft embankment to meet Claypath at a crossroads controlled by traffic lights. The County Authority actually obtained approval from central government, but war intervened. After the war, when the scheme was revived, the City Authority supported Sharp's proposal at a second inquiry, where the Ministry's decision went against the County Authority. The latter's reluctance to accept the decision is the key reason why it took another fifteen years before the relief road and bridges were constructed.[13] The subsequent exponential growth in traffic, if not vindicating the Sharp proposal, certainly highlights the chaos that would have ensued had the County scheme been adopted.

Thomas Sharp was the key figure in averting another disaster for the city, when in 1944 a coal-fired power station was proposed in the vicinity of medieval Kepier Hospital in the valley of the Wear, barely a mile downriver from the

In April 1942 the German Luftwaffe undertook a series of what became known as Baedecker raids, so-called since their targets were not industrial centres but historic towns listed in the German guide book. In quick succession Bath, Exeter and Norwich were bombed, followed by York. Durham seemed an obvious next target.

At 2.30a.m. on 1 May, on a moon-lit night, advanced warning of approaching aircraft was received, and less than half an hour later the air-raid siren sounded. At that point a mist rose from the river valley and covered the whole peninsula. Planes were heard circling overhead but, being unable to locate their target, eventually left, dropping token high explosives at Belmont Grange and Finchale. At 4a.m. the all-clear siren sounded – and the mist dispersed.

The event was reported, and subsequently commented upon, in the local press. Among the witnesses recorded were a member of the Royal Observer Corps and a Home Guard officer, both on duty that night. To those of a sceptical disposition, the river mist was a natural phenomenon, previously observed, the timing of which happened to coincide with the German raid. To those of faith, however, it was a miracle, a miracle almost certainly connected with St Cuthbert. After all, as Symeon recorded, one of the many miracles wrought by St Cuthbert after his death had been a mist he produced to confuse and halt the northern advance of the Conqueror's army in 1069.

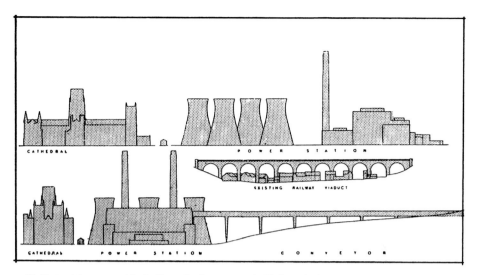

92 Scale of the proposed Kepier Power Station compared with the cathedral and viaduct.

cathedral and a quarter of a mile from a proposed housing development. The dimensions of the proposed so-called cathedral of industry dwarfed those of Norman origin. **(92)** The chimneys were to be 350ft high, the cooling towers 250ft, and both of much wider girth than the cathedral, the central tower of which rises 218ft. The plant would clearly have ruined the green setting of the city, besides being visible from Palace Green. Coal was to arrive via the Gilesgate branch line and a 1,000ft conveyor down into the valley. There was also the question of having to dispose of 350–450 tons of clinker or ash each week. The potential employment for 300 persons in a depressed area was suf-ficient for county and city, coal owners and unions to unite in favour of the project. It was also of sufficient importance for a leading editorial in *The Times*, which argued against the economic rationale two decades before any national conservation lobby had emerged.[14] Sharp argued successfully at the inquiry (on behalf of the Preservation Trust) that it was unnecessary to choose this particu-lar site, which would be environmentally disastrous, both in terms of visual and aerial pollution.

DURHAM RESURGENT

From mid-century new life began to flow through the veins of the city, to the extent that Durham has expanded more since 1950 than in the previous 1,000 years. **(93)** Mobility has been the key. Traditional modes of transport, which formerly facilitated and gave advantage to a concentration of activities, have been replaced by motor transport. The flexibility conferred has allowed a wide choice of location, although at the same time bringing severe challenges to the small historic core.

Traffic flowing north-south no longer had need to enter the city after the construction in the late 1960s of a new Great North Road in the form of a motorway. It passed 2 miles to the east, replacing the former road which for three decades had run through the western outskirts. East-west traffic was facilitated at the same time, and some relief given to the centre, by the building of the relief through road. Demolition associated with the new road could not provide sufficient sites for extra facilities traditionally associated with a city centre, a factor that encouraged movement to out of town industrial estates and retail parks.

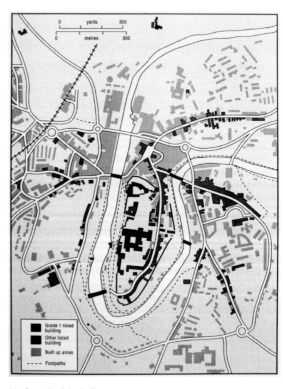

93 Growth of the built-up area.

94 Modern Miners' Gala passing the Royal County Hotel.

A significant event in 1994 was the closure of the county's last colliery, although the industry's memory was kept alive when its annual Gala was converted into a broader TU gathering. The numbers attending declined, being counted in tens, rather than hundreds, of thousands, but all the main ingredients of the festival were retained – parade of banners, bands, speeches, cathedral service – so that once a year the city still takes on its special character. **(94)** For residents, the pageant contrasts with that a week earlier when the parents of graduating students are in town. Indeed, such was the growth of the university, both within the centre and on its extensive estate to the south, that for at least half the year Durham might now be called a university city.

The greater ease of contact made possible by increased mobility was reflected in the major reorganisation of local government areas in 1974, when the small Durham Municipal Borough was logically combined with surrounding Durham Rural District and adjacent Brandon and Byshottles Urban District. The city was now in the centre of the City of Durham District with a combined population of some 80,000, just under half in what was recognised an urban core and over half in some twenty villages around. In 2009, in the most recent reorganisation, the District was abolished and absorbed, along with the county's other five districts, into one, unitary County Authority. The demise of the city as an entity, left initially without even parish status, hardly represented the will of the people.

Opening Up of the City Centre

During the 1960s the central area of the city underwent something akin to open-heart surgery. **(95)** It had long been anticipated, but even after approval of the Sharp scheme it lay on the drawing board for a further decade. Nikolaus Pevsner, in 1953, was among those who looked forward to its realisation, convinced that it would aid the preservation of the city's character, which he found 'more distinctive, more congenial, and at the same time, more alive than many of the older cathedral cities'.[1] Townscape gain, as well as traffic relief, also ensued from the construction of the spur down the Claypath ridge. Sharp had predicted such; architectural critic Ian Nairn immediately concurred, writing that it showed how 'a new road can improve a cathedral city'.[2]

The spur – named Leazes Road – took off from the foot of Gilesgate, where it was joined by a dual-carriageway link from the motorway which, for most of its length, used the railway track of the old NER branch line, closed in 1966. The breaking through of the building line here, and at the foot of Claypath with an underpass, meant that the age-long entry into Durham was no longer confined, and view of the cathedral withheld, until the last moment. The underpass beneath Claypath was undertaken with a degree of demolition that Sharp considered excessive, leaving what he called 'a great hole in the sky'.[3] Despite several different proposals the gap has been narrowed but never closed or

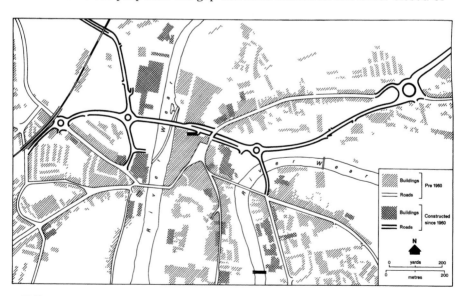

95 New roads and bridges in inner Durham, late 1960s/early 1970s.

96 Through road nearing completion, looking east, early 1970s.

97 Looking east today, along the through road towards Claypath underpass.

healed. **(96, 97)** Sharp hoped that kiosks and shops would link the two parts of severed Claypath and thereby restore the skyline.

The whole project of the inner relief road took nearly twenty years to complete, being undertaken in three phases – Claypath spur and Millburngate Bridge (1963–67), a new Elvet bridge (1968–72) and continuation of the through road from the west bank landfall through a cutting to cross the North Road.

Reinstatement

The west bank was the most extensive area for redevelopment, largely because of the clearance of dilapidated property in the area, which had begun in the 1930s. The first, and most prominent, piece of reinstatement arose at the same time as the bridge was being constructed. Millburngate House, designed by T.F. Winterburn, enclosed a third of a million square feet of office space for the National Savings Certificate headquarters dispersed from London under central government policy. It was fortunate that the location of this large structure of pre-cast concrete units with relief bands of dark grey aggregate was at the lowest point of the river valley – and fortunate also, that Sharp persuaded the authority to omit a thirteen-storey tower. Many may still agree with architectural critic Clifton-Taylor, who summarised it as an 'assertive lump of concrete'.[4]

The west bank on the other side of the bridge saw the emergence of the Millburngate Shopping Centre, now called The Gates. It was constructed in two halves. The first, adjacent to the medieval Framwellgate Bridge into which it is tied, has its mass of brick broken up, an irregular roofline and riverside flats echoing those replaced (Building Design Partnership, 1976). The composition won a Europa Nostra Award for the same year. Its acclaim was widely disseminated through its depiction on a UK postage stamp to commemorate urban renewal. **(98)** The second part (1987), though obviously related, is more ponderous.

The west bank infill in connection with the through road was completed by the colonisation of the sloping ground of Framwellgate Peth below the railway station. On its challenging site a highly successful replication of a Durham Georgian townscape has emerged (R.P. Clouston, 2004). **(99)** The only regret is that the historic name was dropped in favour of Highgate, presumably for marketing purposes.

Further from the bridge downriver a five-storey Raddison Hotel (T. Greenwell, 2008) is respectful, constrained and a highly successful contextual, but not landmark, building.

On the opposite bank the first piece of reinstatement was a brick-faced multi-storey car park, tucked into the back of the Market Place in Leazes Bowl and echoing the old city wall, along which line it followed (William Whitfield, 1975). Unfortunately, this innovatory RIBA-commended structure lasted little more than two decades, for the District Authority, wishing to increase its retail attraction, included the site and the rest of Leazes Bowl in a scheme developed by Boots Property wing (1998) known as the Prince Bishops Shopping Centre – blatantly converted to Prince Bi-Shops in early advertising.

Much more successful was the Millennium Centre (David Prichard, 2003), where a long-derelict site was turned into a distinctive quarter devoted to community uses,

98 Millburngate Centre 1, depicted on a UK postage stamp, 1984.

99 Highgate, built on Framwellgate Peth area, 2004.

100 Millennium Place from Claypath.

most notably a library and theatre. The distinguishing features of the design, chosen from four entries in a competition, are simplicity of line and harmony of materials which reference Durham's vernacular through overhanging eves, clerestory window line and cedar-clad fly-tower of the theatre. **(100)** The site below Millennium Place, latterly occupied by the carpet factory, is Walkergate (Ellis Williams, 2006), another disappointing scheme.

Adjacent to Walkergate downriver Freeman's Quay Leisure Centre (Bottomley, Houldsworth, Saunders, 2008) cleverly brings the downriver spread of Walkergate to an end. Its broad, sloping roof, overriding the curve of wall enclosing the pool, comes to rest on a colonnade of bevelled concrete columns. It is a building of distinction.

The Market Place could hardly be reinstated, but the exclusion of through traffic opened the way for partial pedestrianisation – partial, since Saddler Street is the only vehicular route to the cathedral and colleges on the peninsula, while properties lining the narrow streets between the Market Place and the two medieval bridges have no rear access for servicing. A compromise scheme restricted the servicing of commercial premises to early and late parts of the day, while introduction of a congestion charge in 2002, in what was described as the country's first toll road in modern times, considerably reduced vehicular traffic onto the peninsula.

A floorscaping scheme was introduced immediately following pedestrianisation. Designed by the city's planning officer, Anthony Scott (1977), it was entirely in keeping with the medieval streets and Market Place. Secondhand sandstone flags and blocks, with central concrete wheelers, united the two sides of the street and evoked continuity with the past. **(101)** It gave unity to the historic

101 Floorscaping, Silver Street, 1978.

centre, which in 1968 had been made one of the first Conservation Areas in the country. In 1992 Neptune was restored and returned to the Market Place. His homecoming, however, was soon to be disturbed, for in less than two decades both he and the equestrian statue of Lord Londonderry were to be moved in a highly contentious modern makeover.

Outward Movement

The movement of activities to the periphery of Durham long preceded that caused or encouraged by the city's through road. The County Hospital, for instance, had moved to its Dryburn site in the 1940s. The County Authority moved nearby, onto the Aykley Heads Estate after vacating its premises in Old Elvet. Appropriately, the new six-storey block was designed by one of its own staff (J.J.S. Dixon, 1963). A year later the police headquarters made the identical transfer from the end of Old Elvet to Aykley Heads. A notable accompaniment alongside the new station was a 150ft high, ultra-thin, reinforced concrete radio mast, designed by Ove Arup. It was subsequently given listed building status. One further removal that was considered at one point was the gaol. In fact, its need remained; moreover an additional gaol was required, and

built at Frankland, 2 miles to the north-east. Two senior schools also relocated on the periphery.

Motor transport characteristically gave rise to out-of-town estates – industrial, business and retail – with the grouping of similar or related activities. Durham was no exception. Its largest estates were located with access to the motorway (Belmont and Dragonville to the east, Bowburn in the south) or at Meadowfield (on the A690 westwards.) Manufactures were of the lighter variety, such as plastics, television components, containers, food and drink. Government incentives were often critical; their change or withdrawal could mean that some stays proved to be temporary.

Two notable companies that moved to industrial estates were the carpet and organ factories. The former, which lost part of its Freeman's Place site to the new through road, continued to expand here until the late 1960s, when lack of further space caused it to look elsewhere. The first transfer to Dragonville occurred in 1970; ten years later the whole plant had been relocated. The company, which received a royal warrant in 1972, continued the tradition of concentrating on the middle and upper market, despite the rise elsewhere of cheaper synthetic carpets. Their carpets graced public buildings, hotels, liners, even palaces. The new county hall foyer and council chamber, naturally, were carpeted with the local product. In terms of employment, the figure rose sharply in the 1970s to exceed 800, but then equally rapid decline set in. Subsequent changes in type of demand, foreign competition and then, critically, a cash crisis in 2005 brought an end to a famous company.

The organ factory moved out to a purpose-built workshop on the Meadowfield Estate in 1997. Its reputation and output has continued to grow. At home, new organs include those for Coventry Cathedral and the Royal Festival Hall. Abroad, the company was responsible for the organ in Stockholm City Hall, in which the Nobel Prize ceremonies are held, while further afield organs have been shipped across the Atlantic and to South-East Asia and Australasia.

Large retail parks have also been established to the north (Arnison Centre) and east (Sunderland Road). Supermarket chains and bulky goods were the first obvious occupants, but subsequent expansion of a wide range of outlets has added to their attraction, which has had inevitable repercussions on the city centre. More recently some service activities – solicitors, insurance, newspaper office – have also taken flight to a peripheral business park, thereby further eroding the variety in the city centre. The provision of three park-and-ride sites on the periphery has, however, eased congestion in the centre, which, unlike many towns, continues to exert an environmental attraction in its own right.

University City

For the first 120 years the university remained a small institution, with student numbers counted in hundreds. From 1950, in which year the total reached 1,000 for the first time, numbers began to increase significantly. In fact, such was the acceleration in numbers that within twenty years *Northern Architect* could boldly state that 'first and foremost Durham is a university city'.[5] A series of what were intended to be long-term development plans – 1947, 1952, 1969 – had to be revised as previous projections were exceeded. In the most comprehensive of the three plans, that by William Whitfield and Brian Hackett in 1969, a total figure of 6,000 students was estimated for the year 2000. Anything more, they considered, was incompatible with the size of the city.[6] That maximum figure was exceeded long before the end of the century; today it is approaching 13,000.

In the early 1960s the idea of developing as a 'campus' institution was abandoned when the opportunity arose to acquire Old Shire Hall and several Georgian townhouses opposite in Old Elvet, which the county council vacated for its new site at Aykley Heads. There was even a suggestion that in the long term the nearby gaol could also become university property. Teaching blocks for arts disciplines were built on obsolete buildings in New Elvet, while science departments located half a mile to the south, thereby confirming the original 1924 location of the Dawson Building. The growth of sciences was important for Durham after the ending of the federal status of the two institutions in 1960 when Newcastle, which possessed the major science faculties, achieved independent status. The retention of the park-like landscape to the south for the dispersed location of new colleges was a key principal of the first Development Plan.

In the first part of this period the university commissioned several distinguished architects to design parts of the rapidly expanding institution. Sir Derman Christopherson, vice-chancellor 1960–79 and later chairman of the Royal Fine Art Commission, was a key figure here. Among the notable additions to the city was that created by George Pace. His brief was certainly the most daunting challenge: to insert a large new university library on Palace

Green between two of the most famous pieces of historic architecture in the country. The result (1966), according to contemporary critic Patrick Nuttgens, was 'one of the most brilliant examples of modern buildings in old surroundings'.[7] The genius of the stone-clad building is that it does not front onto Palace Green, from where it is hardly visible, but is perched on Broken Walls, from where it can be appreciated. Its special context is best seen from South Street.

George Pace was also consultant architect to the cathedral (1954–71), in which role he was extremely active. In each of his numerous works – from candlesticks and an inscription behind Bede's tomb, to undercroft restaurant and bookshop, to wrought-iron gates for the deanery and its external staircase – here was an architect in tune with the spirit of place. The contextual appropriateness of his design in general was best summed up by a critic who had visited his works exhibited at the Royal Academy: 'He takes infinite pains to ensure what he has in mind is right as he sees it, not for George Pace, not for the sake of an argument, not to indicate a method, but for Durham.'[8]

A second notable building, Dunelm House (1963), home of the Students' Union, is strikingly innovative. A strong building guarding entry to the gorge section of the river, it is the city's only example of brutalist architecture. Its dramatic sculptural form echoes in concrete several of the idioms of the city's vernacular architecture – fragmentation, irregular fenestration, overlapping pantiles and, on the street side, cantilevered storeys. It forms a single composition with Kingsgate Bridge (1963), a taut high-level footbridge exploiting the high ribbed vault of the cathedral, eliminating everything except the ribs themselves. **(102)** The resultant townscape composition was described by Douglass Wise as 'the greatest contribution modern architecture has made to the enjoyment of an English medieval city'.[9]

Michael Powers was the architect for the house, Ove Arup the structural engineer and architectural adviser. For the bridge Ove Arup was both designer and structural engineer. It is humbling to reflect that, despite his imaginative solutions for Sydney Opera House, the Pompidou Centre, Barbican and Coventry Cathedral, he nevertheless considered Kingsgate Bridge to be his favourite piece. This was commemorated in a special way when, on the day of his private family funeral in London in February 1988, wreaths were laid on their master's bridge from all twenty of his UK offices. **(103)** A more lasting acknowledgement is a portrait head of the great man on Dunelm House looking down on his bridge, which, along with the first Severn crossing, is the only GradeI listed modern bridge in the country.

102 Dunelm House and Kingsgate Bridge.

103 Wreaths laid on Kingsgate Bridge in memory of Sir Ove Arup.

104 St Chad's College extension, 1964.

Another noteworthy addition was the fusing of old and new by Francis Johnson (1964) in a large expansion of St Chad's College in the North Bailey opposite the east end of the cathedral. **(104)** The architect was presented with a low cottage at the corner of Bow Lane and a sequence of four eighteenth-century townhouses along the Bailey. Although conservation was hardly in vogue at the time, Johnson retained the street elevation of the townhouses to one room in depth, linking them to new construction behind. On the corner he designed a dining hall and kitchen, with student rooms above. Externally it forms a prominent, but not dominant, conclusion to the sequence of the former Georgian houses, while the light brown brick reflects the stone of the cathedral opposite. It is intriguing to speculate whether its attractive, slightly curved ogee front, which might be read as hinting at a bishop's mitre, is intended humour, since the college at the time contained within it a 'High Church' theological seminary. Perhaps this is what Archbishop Ramsey had in mind when, at the opening, he remarked that 'Mr Johnson has been very ingenious here, almost indecently so.'[10]

Six university colleges were set in parkland to the south, each by a different architect in a different idiom. St Aidan's College (Sir Basil Spence, 1965) is set on a knoll, and is a monumental essay of solids and voids incorporating clichés from the architect's work elsewhere. **(105)** Trevelyan College (H. Stillman and J. Eastwick-Field, 1967), lower down and in lightly wooded land with a glimpse of the cathedral, is a hexagonal composition that draws its imagination from the keep of the castle. **(106)** Van Mildert College (P. Middleton, 1966) exploits its small lake with flanking serrated blocks and cloistered walk of exceptional quality. Collingwood College (Sir Richard Shepherd, 1973) interlaces brick massing and mature trees. St Mary's College (V. Harris, 1952) stands clear on the lower slopes of the park landscape, with the clearest view of the cathedral, and is a monumental conception with a clear hint of a French chateau. Of these early buildings only Grey College (T. Worthington, 1961), with an emasculated Georgian style of an inflated domestic form, can be said to disappoint.

The extent of new building reflected the rapid growth of the institution. By 1970 the student number had reached 3,500, then, after a pause, climbed fast, especially in the 1990s, to attain 12,700 by 2012. Almost all colleges built extensions; only two new colleges were established – Ustinov (2000) and Josephine Butler (both Gotch, Surridge & Saunders, 2006) towards the southern extremity of the university estate. The institution was indeed fortunate to possess an estate of some 590 acres.

105 St Aidan's College, 1965.

106 Trevelyan College, 1967.

With the Science Site departments expanding commensurately, it was evident that the university's centre of gravity was moving southwards. This was acknowledged when the university's main library was transferred to the Science Site (H. Faulkner-Brown, 1983, extended 1994) and then confirmed in the *University Master Plan and Development Framework, 2006*. The key movement was the vacating of Old Shire Hall for a new administrative centre (Pereira, Hodgson and Grounsell, 2012), an overpowering building fronting Stockton Road, no more sympathetic to its surroundings than was the shire hall when built. The remainder of the university's townhouses in Old Elvet are also being gradually vacated.

With over 12,000 students, and some 3,800 employed as teaching, support and service staff, the university now plays a critical role in the life and economy of the city. Durham certainly is a university city, for it easily has the highest percentage of students among its residents of any town in England.

One significant change amid the growth has been in the proportion of students living in colleges, from approaching three-quarters in 1970 to well under half today. Those students living out of college number nearly 5,500 occupying well over 1,200 properties, the overwhelming majority of which were formerly private residences. In the vicinity of the rail viaduct some dozen streets have more than nine-tenths of houses in student occupation. Here, and in some other parts of the city, the change wrought by the process of so-called 'studentification' has brought into question the whole problem of sustained and balanced communities. While the university was unable to provide accommodation commensurate with the increase in student numbers, at the same time it appears that planners were taken by surprise and were too slow to react. In consequence, the social geography of some parts of the city has been changed for the foreseeable future.

UNIVERSITY CHANCELLORS

The saying 'Durham is different' was recently used in the title of a book commissioned by the university to recount its history. The antecedence and evolution of England's third university has certainly been distinctive. In most recent times one element of this characteristic can be seen in the choice of chancellors. Whereas other institutions elect diplomats, statesmen, dukes, and so on, Durham has looked to the world of arts. Each has brought distinction and colour, exemplifying how art can transcend the conventional.

The first, Dame Margot Fonteyn (1981–90), one of the greatest classical ballet dancers of all time, brought grace and consummate professionalism to the role – appearing to express the poetry of the place. The ballroom in Dunelm House was renamed in her honour. Sir Peter Ustinov (1992–2004), actor, writer, dramatist, humorist and much more, was already an ambassador on the world stage for UNICEF and the World Federalist Movement before taking on his ambassadorial role for the university. The university's postgraduate college was renamed in his honour.

Author Bill Bryson (2005–11) could hardly decline his invitation, having written in *Notes from a Small Island* that Durham was 'a perfect little city' and urging anyone who had not seen it to go at once – even to the extent of taking his car. An indication of his care for the city's environment was his immediate life membership of the local civic amenity society. He was already a commissioner for English Heritage, and became president of CPRE. Sir Thomas Allen (2012–) is one of the best lyrical baritones of his era, with a repertoire from opera to songs from his native North East. As a County Durham man, he will bring a special understanding to representing the university on the wider stage.

ten

A WORLD HERITAGE SITE

N o one can fail to be impressed with the dramatic skyline of the peninsula acropolis, even if its cultural significance is unknown. It has its Michelin stars and Baedecker recommendation; its European standing was confirmed by Pevsner; its world rank has come from such diverse sources as Ruskin and Bryson. Not the least noteworthy here is the result of the ballot by the Royal Institute of British Architects, held at the time of its 150th anniversary in 1984, in which Durham Cathedral was voted the 'best building in the world'.[1] It was hardly a surprise, therefore, that the cathedral and castle received official World Heritage status in 1986.

The UK government did not ratify the 1972 World Convention until 1984, as a result of which it became eligible to nominate sites from a national list of possibilities. Durham was in the first batch of seven sites put forward, and was inscribed on the UNESCO world list in November 1986.

World Heritage Site: Boundary Delimitation

In 1985 scant attention was paid to boundaries: all emphasis was on getting the documentation ready to include Durham Cathedral and castle in the first batch of submissions. The survey of the site was hardly thorough, for the person dispatched by the Historic Buildings Commission to assemble the case was unacquainted with Durham, stayed only two days and considered it unnecessary to consult the city or county planning departments. Meanwhile, the dean and vice-chancellor had been given less than a fortnight to reply to a letter from the Department of Environment, received without warning, to confirm that they saw no objections to including the cathedral and castle on the UK's 'Tentative List'.

The site inscribed in November 1986 was split-site, with boundaries drawn around the two buildings. **(107)** Even judged by its own terms of reference, the delimitation was inconsistent. The area considered to be the cathedral and former abbey precinct incorporated parts that had always been outside. At the southern end the eighteenth-century Prebends' Bridge was tacked on as a narrow appendage.

In 2008 the World Heritage body agreed to an extension of the site by incorporating Palace Green, thereby uniting the two elements. The bailey was made the eastern boundary for the whole of its length. The historic integrity and cohesiveness of the site was thereby acknowledged, as was the inclusion of non-monumental buildings. The castle and 'half castle 'gainst the Scot', the palace and cathedral, belong together and are linked by Palace Green, which was not only the processional route between the two but was flanked by a series of diocesan buildings, from courthouse to almshouses.

While the case for inclusion of Palace Green was incontrovertible, the bailey is unsatisfactory as a divide from the point of view of history or townscape, while Prebends' Bridge remains an isolated addition. A larger, coherent unit that retains all the essential features of the World Heritage Site can be shown to be at hand.

The near-encircling river and its steep riverbanks form a collar embracing the walled citadel. It is both the complement to, and intimately linked with, the settlement above. The river has been a means of defence – a moat writ large – and water power. Its banks have been quarries for building stone, a line of defence, orchards, gardens, a place for promenading. It is the defile that gives the peninsula, the 'hill-island', its dramatic skyline. A boundary along the top of the outer bank would be uncomplicated in outline or in terms of land ownership. The two medieval bridges, Framwellgate and Elvet, provide obvious 'stops'

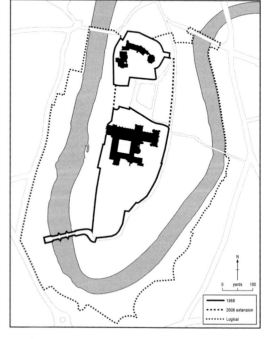

107 Boundaries of the World Heritage Site.

and serve the same role as Prebends' Bridge in providing memorable views of the cathedral and castle. **(108, 109)**

The symbiosis just outlined fully conforms with UNESCO's World Heritage emblem, which 'symbolizes the interdependence of cultural and natural properties: the central square is a form created by man and the circle represents nature, the two being intimately linked. The emblem is round like the world, but at the same time it is a symbol of protection.' **(110)**

From the point of view of Durham's World Heritage status, the extension would not dilute the original three criteria justifying its designation by UNESCO, nor from the eight separate components deriving from these criteria and listed by the International Council on Monuments and Sites.

Outstanding Universal Value of the Site

The values by which Durham is judged to derive its 'Outstanding Universal Value' may be summarised thus:

The exceptional architecture demonstrating architectural innovation.

The visual drama of the cathedral and castle on the peninsula, and the associations with notions of romantic beauty.

The physical expression of the spiritual and secular powers of the medieval Bishops Palatine that the defended complex provides.

The relics and material culture of the three saints (Cuthbert, Bede and Oswald) buried at the site.

The continuity of use and ownership over the past 1,000 years as a place of religious worship, learning and residence.

Its role as a political statement of Norman power imposed upon a subjugate nation, as one of the country's most powerful symbols of the Norman Conquest of Britain.

The importance of its archaeological remains, which are directly related to its history and continuity of use over the past 1,000 years.

The cultural and religious traditions and historical memoirs associated with the relics of St Cuthbert and the Venerable Bede, and with the continuity of use and ownership over the past millennium.

Many of the above points will have surfaced during the telling of the story of Durham thus far. The reader is therefore asked to forgive any repetition, for the collective retelling of the points will highlight the international or global importance of a small city.

The cathedral is the largest and most perfect monument of Norman architecture in the county. It is a building by which others are judged. Internationally it represents 'the ultimate fulfilment of that tendency towards articulation which had driven Romanesque architects forward for over a hundred years'.[2] As the earliest surviving completely ribbed vaulted church, demonstrating the value of the pointed arch, it was an experimental innovation far ahead of its time. In contrast to the billowing vaults of the cathedral is the subterranean chapel in the castle, a catacomb space deemed to mark a turning point in the evolution of eleventh-century Romanesque sculpture.

111 The view from Prebends' Bridge.

The cathedral and castle are the physical expression of the Norman Conquest of this country and, subsequently, of the spiritual and secular powers of Bishops Palatine, a line installed by the conquerors to be the monarch's viceroy in the region.

The same dramatic skyline of cathedral and castle on the peninsula, rising above the river and wooded banks, is an aesthetic highlight. It is a composition that varies with the viewer's position, as well as by season and time of day – or night. Travellers, writers and artists have long been attracted, most notably from the second half of the eighteenth century with the rise of the picturesque tour and notions of romantic landscape. At this time the banks were landscaped, paths laid out and Prebends' Bridge intentionally repositioned. The view from the last-named has become one of the most famous views in England. **(111)**

Pevsner assessed the prospect from the bridge as 'the most moving' from which to view 'one of the great architectural experiences of Europe'.[3] Turner was 'moved' to wrestle with the spirit of place – the *genius loci* of Durham – in his lyrical rendering of the scene in 1835, more than three decades after his first visit. **(112)** The cathedral is turned almost forty-five degrees and in the ethereal colouring of the late afternoon light appears to be rising from the rock on which it is set. Its overwhelming prominence also accords well with our memory in the mind's eye.[4] The contrived lines of the left-hand trees, distant Framwellgate

Bridge, weir and Prebends' Bridge parapet all lead the eye to the three towers to complete the spiritual symbolism of the picture.

Associated with the cathedral, the former abbey church is the most complete pre-Dissolution monastery in the country, both in its claustral buildings and in its outer courtyard, now called The College. Exceptional spaces are the dormitory, refectory library and great kitchen. (The stone-vaulted kitchen is one of only two known to survive in the whole of Europe.) Even the Georgian prebendal houses in the outer courtyard often conceal much medieval fabric within.

The county's largest collection of pre-Dissolution manuscripts is also housed here. Pre-eminent are the seventh-century *Durham Gospels*, which would be an artistic rival to the *Lindisfarne Gospels* were it not damaged, although perhaps the *St Cuthbert Gospel* now deserves the highest mention. Recently acquired by the British Library after an appeal, it is to spend half of its time that it is on display in Durham. It was written in the last years of the seventh century, and still has its original red goatskin binding complete with incised decorations. Having escaped rebinding, the volume is therefore the oldest intact European book. It was buried with St Cuthbert in 698, and rediscovered when the coffin was opened in 1104 on the translation of St Cuthbert's body to the present feretory. It was taken from Durham at the Reformation. (The late seventh-century *Lindisfarne Gospels*, this country's earliest surviving great masterpiece of

112 'Durham Cathedral', watercolour by J.M.W. Turner, 1835.

A World Heritage Site is a large artefact or locality inscribed on the UNESCO World Heritage list, which dates from 1972. The genesis was two-fold, relating to the cultural and natural environments. Thus, on the one hand, there was the concern generated by the rescue efforts of the Nubian sculptures from the rising waters of the Nile, the 1966 floods in Florence and the winter flooding of Venice. On the other, there was the experience gained from the United Nation's Environmental Programme and conferences on National Parks.

The UNESCO conference of 1972 set up a World Heritage Committee to identify, protect and conserve for the benefit of mankind as a whole material heritage of 'outstanding universal value'. Nominations were to be the initiative of countries that had signed the 1972 Convention, submitted from a Tentative List prepared in the light of issued guidelines. The submitted documents accompanying an application were to be evaluated by a cultural or environmental committee and the decision passed to the World Heritage Committee, and finally to UNESCO.

The first batch of a dozen sites was inscribed in 1978; the number is now well over 900. The UK ratified the Convention in 1984, having delayed for political reasons. Durham was among the first clutch of seven submissions inscribed in 1986, being recorded as number 370 on the List. The UK (Great Britain and its overseas territories) currently has twenty-eight sites, twenty-three being cultural, one natural and one mixed), with a further thirteen on its Tentative List. The latter includes the joint monastery of Monkwearmouth-Jarrow.

medieval book painting, was similarly removed and is now permanently in the British Library.)

There are also no fewer than three copies of the Magna Carta. The music library, beginning after the founding of the chorister school in the early fifteenth century, is nationally renowned. Significant also is Cosin's seventeenth-century library, not only for its content but also for its innovative design. Cosin's part in shaping the 1662 Book of Common Prayer is also evident in one of the deposits, with much annotation in his own handwriting on a revision draft.

The important collections of books stem from Durham being a centre of education and learning throughout its history – Cuthbert Community, Benedictines, Durham College in Oxford, through to the founding of the university.

The cathedral is also important for possessing the remains not of one saint but three – Cuthbert, Bede, Oswald – and for the relics and material culture associated with them. Pre-eminent among them are Cuthbert's carved wooden coffin, within which was found, along with his body, his pectoral cross, a portable altar and ivory comb, along with medieval vestments and embroidery presented to the shrine by King Athelstan in the tenth century, the latter being among the oldest surviving examples in Europe.

A factor undergirding several of the above attributes contributing to the significance in world heritage terms has been the continuity of use and ownership over the past 1,000 years. It has been, and remains, a place of religious worship, learning and residence. The World Heritage Site, then, is very much a living community, besides being a centre of pilgrimage, both religious and tourist. In the latter role, a World Heritage Visitor Centre has recently been created in restored almshouses in Owengate at the entrance to Palace Green, while special exhibition spaces have been created in the University Library on Palace Green. The cathedral itself is currently in the early stage of a series of projects, aptly named Open Treasure, aiming to transform the way in which both cathedral and former monastery buildings are experienced, understood and used. Nothing so momentous has occurred since the work of restorers and 'improvers' during the reign of Queen Victoria.

eleven

DURHAM DISTILLED

THE QUALITY OF 'DURHAMNESS'

Having turned the pages of Durham's story, there remains the task of distilling the essence of the city: of explicating the quality of what might be termed 'Durhamness'. For this, one must combine the outsider's curiosity with the insider's love.

What then is Durham? In summary, it is an aesthetic high, an architectural innovation, a cultural benchmark.[1] Durham is a visual delight, attractive from a great variety of angles. It is also where the structural thrust problem in major buildings was resolved, where the rib-vault, buttress and pointed arch of the Gothic were first demonstrated. Again, Durham is the nation's monument to the Norman invasion, the last invasion of this country. Here, the Normans confirmed a site chosen for, or by, the North's most famous saint. It is a physical manifestation of a story, a story with a quality of legend concerning St Cuthbert. Moreover, history and story have been certified for us in writings, verse and painting. No landscape, it may be held, is truly rich until it has been certified in this manner, and particularly so when the story has the quality of legend or myth.

In recent times the recording has been in terms of official ranking or statutory listing: its Conservation Area was early recognised and classed as 'outstanding'; it is on the select list of National Heritage Towns drawn up by the British Council of Archaeology; and it is, of course, a UNESCO World Heritage Centre. In consequence, Durham is assuredly somewhere, and the person from somewhere is someone. As a place with identity, it reinforces our identity.

The distinctiveness of Durham's identity is associated with the fact that surprise infuses the key constituent elements. Size may well be the first element to call forth surprise, for if the cathedral has been taken as the touchstone of size, then one is certainly expecting something much bigger. The rail traveller in particular will have been misled. **(113)** The cathedral bestows the

113 View from Wharton Park above the railway station.

114 View towards Durham, 2 miles to the east. St Nicholas's church and the viaduct are clearly visible, besides the cathedral and castle.

appellation 'city' to the settlement, but the urban form and accompanying facilities are surprisingly modest.

Boundedness is a related second element. **(114)** The city is a distinct identity; it does not fray at the edges; it does not stutter into being through suburbia. The suddenness of arrival reinforces this perception. Given the speed of modern travel, it is almost possible to believe that town and country meet at a line as abrupt as in medieval times. The cathedral, as a marker, may initially beckon from afar – perhaps 8 to 10 miles distant – but it is then hidden until the last minute as one reaches or breaches the rim of the basin in which it is set. The particular routes taken by major entries through the surrounding teasing topography play their part in this experience.

The architectural climax of cathedral together with castle on a raised river-girt peninsula is, of course, the most memorable feature, a silhouette widely projected as the city's visual signature – or icon in present terminology. Within the climax the cathedral is the tallest, grandest building on the highest site, rising as high as the river incision is deep below. It is a crowning, dramatic climax. On

arrival, the visitor is in no doubt that there is a there there. For the community it is also the social anchor point, the focus for a myriad of diverse gatherings.

The surrounding townscape is in complete contrast to the climax, being domestic in scale, organic in layout and varied in age. **(115, 116)** It rises and falls, winds and staggers as if in sympathy with river course and topography. There is coherence and legibility, but not one of instant revelation, for that way boredom lies. There is certainly no street called 'Straight', no layout easily conforming to the psychologist's 'good figure'. (Neither is the winding river a reliable guide in this respect, with no obvious left and right bank and flow masked by weirs. The American novelist Nathaniel Hawthorne cannot be the only one to have been confused.[2] In Durham it is a richer experience, not to be rushed, one that comes with effort from following a series of intriguing beckonings, with the changing silhouette of cathedral and castle frequently providing orientation to which one can turn or return for assurance.

An official measure of the quality of the townscape can be gauged from the number of listed buildings, for there are no fewer than 600 properties in the city's central area classified as being of 'special architectural or historic interest' on the Secretary of State's countrywide register. When plotted on a map their distribution, not surprisingly, strongly correlates with early maps of the city,

115 South Street.

116 South Bailey.

with listed buildings lining its historic entries. **(117)**

Greenness is a final all-pervading quality. This consists of more than the regulatory provision of open space, urbanised manicured parkland or tree-lined streets. The countryside, even the working countryside, approaches and appears to enter the heart of the city. Even closer are St Margaret's Allotments, off leafy Margery Lane, with the cathedral rising behind. **(118)** This particular view here is Durham's equivalent of Constable's Salisbury Cathedral from the water meadows. The

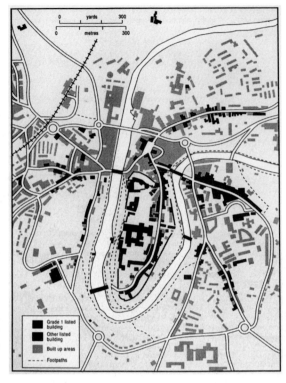

117 Listed buildings in central Durham.

contrast in terms of aesthetics and social worlds is surprising only to outsiders; for insiders it is part of the accepted order: part of Durham. We may also be aware of the symbolic value of the allotment site, for as our faith tells us we originated in a garden, so did our cathedral originate from stone dug in this garden. Marked on some early maps as the abbey fishpond, the bowl-shape configuration betrays its original role as a quarry.

Not the least contribution to the greenness of Durham is the broad wedge that accompanies the river on its entire course through the city. Below the peninsula's plateau, through the castle wall, the riverbanks present a different world. Although most obviously a green haven, they are in effect a world where daily and seasonal variations bring an ever-changing mood. The contrast between the plateau and the snow-covered banks, with a gas-lit lamp at the junction, is said to have inspired C.S. Lewis, here in the winter of 1943, to conceive of the entrance to the fictional world of Narnia. According to the author, the opening scene of a faun carrying an umbrella and parcels in a snowy wood had been a picture in his head for some five years.[3] W.H. Lewis, who accompanied his brother on his visit to Durham, wrote in his *Diaries* that the beauty of the cathedral town and its stupendous setting on the banks of the Wear took

118 St Margaret's
Allotments.

119 Riverbank interest:
Kathedra sculpture by Colin
Wilbourn.

120 Riverbank interest:
the former cornmill
seen through the arch of
Prebends' Bridge.

121 View south from the cathedral tower.

122 View to the city centre from Observatory Hill.

123 View to the city centre from Flass Vale.

both of them by marvellous surprise.[4] (The smallness of the university was the inspiration, though not model, for the small northern university of Edgestow in his novel *That Hideous Strength*, which appeared two years later.)

Dispersed within the green wedge of the riverbanks is the added interest of medieval wells and mills, an eighteenth-century ice house and summer house, besides, of course, views which, as Thomas Gray found, change 'every ten steps'. **(119, 120)** The view from Prebends' Bridge, with the cathedral rising from the banks of trees, may be the classic view, but if one allows the eye to be led downstream the compactness of the settlement is revealed, for at one and the same time the observer is looking towards the heart of the city centre and to the countryside beyond. It is a characteristic that from many parts of the middle of the city one can lift up one's eyes and see not only the cathedral but the rim with its green skyline. In reverse, the panorama from the top of the cathedral tower will confirm that the greenness is no trick of inter-visibility. **(121)**

The rim of the bowl in which the city is set provides confirmation of its green setting from all points of the compass – from Pelaw Wood, Old Durham, Shincliffe, Mount Joy, Windmill Hill, Observatory Hill, **(122)** Flass Vale, **(123)** Aykley Heads, Kepier. All have attracted, and been recorded by, a succession of artists.[5] The precious nature of these so-called 'long views' is given its most emphatic endorsement by Alec Clifton-Taylor: 'at Durham, nothing, absolutely and positively nothing, must ever be permitted to intrude upon the great views'.[6]

The ecclesiastical authorities showed their dedicated concern when Dean Heaton purchased a strip of land on the upper approaches to the railway station in the 1920s solely in order to remove advertisement hoardings and thus restore the view of the city for the benefit of rail travellers. The general care of the environment exercised by the ecclesiastical authority is shown not only in this act, or in conservation of its buildings, but also in its 'banksmen', who plant, prune, repair and daily remove litter in service to the quality of place.

The various elements described combine together to constitute the quality of 'Durhamness'. The distinctiveness – the surprising distinctiveness – however, derives not only from the heightened degree to which elements are present, but from the co-existence of opposing qualities. A series of dualities, holding in tension two opposites, can be recognised. Thus Durham is spiritual and secular. It has at its heart cathedral and castle. Even the cathedral itself, to repeat again Sir Walter Scott's well-known words, is 'Half church of God, half castle 'gainst

Artists, as the antennae of the race, have continued in modern times to respond in new ways to the challenge of St Cuthbert and Durham Cathedral, many of the most memorable coming from those who have had long acquaintance.

Among writers, Bill Bryson penned the ultimate accolade with his comment 'best cathedral on planet Earth'. Among painters, none has surpassed the drama and mystery captured in the interior scenes by Sunderland-born Birtley Aris, not least in the perspectives from triforium and clerestory. Local resident Janie Bickersteth has been intrigued by the massiveness and patterning of the pillars. The latter has been among the subjects studied during two decades of a cathedral artist residency, a joint cathedral-university venture, which allowed an artist to spend a year interacting with the cathedral.

Sculptor Fenwick Lawson, who for several years has lived in the shadow of the cathedral, has long been attracted to Cuthbert. Working in wood, he allows the grain to bring movement – to release the form – not least in his 'Cuthbert of Farne', carved from an elm that had grown by the north entrance to the cathedral. Below the Celtic swirls and drapery, a cuddy duck sits at the feet of the contemplative monk. After several years in the cathedral cloister it needed restoration before returning to the city's Heritage Centre, but not before a bronze cast was made for Lindisfarne.

The sculptor then produced 'The Journey', six full-size monks bearing the coffin of St Cuthbert on their journey from Lindisfarne to Durham, which stands in Millennium Place. Most recently a Wheel Cross, carved with references to Lindisfarne and Durham, has been erected in the centre. It was originally intended to be one of a series, marking halts in the epic journey over many years.

A musical response to St Cuthbert is the oratorio by Durham-born Will Todd, with words by Ben Dunwell. The ten-movement poem, drawing on ancient scripts and liturgies, recounts Cuthbert's life and events after his death, culminating with his arrival in Durham. As an art form, it expresses most deeply the *genius loci*.

Cuthbert, then, remains a source of pilgrimage and wonder. It was appropriate, therefore, that the saint's name, removed from the designation of the cathedral at the Reformation, should have been recently restored alongside Christ and the Blessed Virgin Mary to an inspiring building erected in his honour.

the Scot'. Again, Durham is nature and culture. It is town and country. 'Town and country must be married', wrote Ebenezer Howard a century ago. Here the marriage does not consist of thousands of units, each in its own plot, as in his garden cities, but rather is a city in a garden, a large temple in the middle of the greenery.

Durham is also monumentalism and the domestic. It speaks of master masons with international ideas and of more modest craftsmen and the vernacular. Durham is committed to one time period, yet is timeless in what it proclaims. As the capital of the county it belongs to the folk of the county, who have considerable pride in their town: we are Cuthbert's people or Cuddy's folk. Yet Durham belongs to British history, western civilisation, the whole of Christendom.

There is therefore a degree of apartness, even aloofness. In the very beginning, for instance, the city did not evolve out of a relationship with the surrounding countryside: it was planted by Saxon pilgrims and confirmed by the conquering Normans. After centuries of only moderate pretence as a market centre, the city remained aloof from the Industrial Revolution and was almost unscarred by coal-mining, despite being in the geographical centre of the extensive coalfield. During the peak of landscape disfigurement Sharp described the remarkable contrast in terms of the cathedral city being 'a flower among the filth';[7] Priestley, who drew travellers' attention to the attractive view of the city from the railway, advised them not to alight for fear of revulsion at the mining landscapes around.[8]

Other factors have compounded the characteristic of being in, but not of, the area. The university, for instance, is today decidedly national, or international, not local or provincial in orientation. A (former) perceived reluctance to turn the distinguished microscope of scholarship on its home area caused novelist Sid Chaplin to refer to the students and teachers as 'colonialists' and the institution as 'stuck in the county's crop'.[9] The city's employment structure as a whole is quite unrepresentative of the region in which it is set. In fact, the city is set apart in any table of averages, be they economic, social or political.

Durham, then, is different, with an apartness that transcends local or national significance, yet at the same time speaking to each one of us, both in reminding us of our story while pointing to lasting values. A paradox, a not inappropriate conclusion for a city that has a paradox enshrined at its centre: St Cuthbert, a hermit and contemplative by inclination, who drew to himself people and preferment.

twelve

THE FUTURES OF DURHAM

C hange is the one constant in this world, even for towns we call historic. The passage of time brings inexorable change – from the physical process of erosion, through nature's growth and decay to, most notably, the increasing social and technological intervention of humankind. 'Futures' is in the plural, for change can vary in both pace and direction.[1]

While change is inexorable, questions are asked of it by conservation. In fact, conservation may be defined as the management of change. Hence the definition given by English Heritage: 'The process of managing change to a significant place in its setting in ways that will best sustain its heritage values, while recognising opportunities to reveal or reinforce those values for present and future generations.'[2]

Durham is decidedly a 'significant place'. Its components have been described, their story told and the quality of Durhamness outlined. The touch-stone of successful management of change, therefore, is whether the quality of Durhamness is preserved or enhanced. If this test is applied, then many individual structures in the last half century have undoubtedly enriched the townscape, but some recent, prominent ones have fallen short, while several consultants' reports and even local authority proposals give rise to some anxiety. It is important that the reasons for such anxiety are understood.

The first of three recent schemes that may be cited as falling short is the Prince Bishops Centre (1998). The placing of a large retail development on top of a multi-storey car park on land that falls steeply away from the back of the Market Place has resulted in monstrous external elevations that drop vertically to both riverside and Leazes Road. The latter elevation, illustrated here, shows no respect for the context into which it was inserted, either in terms of site or architecture. A comparison of the townscape that was lost reveals the extent to which the intrusion is alien. **(124, 125)** The local authority was culpable in

124 Before: the view to the cathedral car park from back Claypath, 1980.

125 After: the view to Prince Bishops Centre from back Claypath, today.

that it turned a blind eye to its own Design Brief, which took full account of the topography of the site.

A second disappointment is Walkergate (2006), which was intended to be complementary to Millennium Place in its uses and to relate in terms of its architecture. It succeeds on the first front, as a series of food and drink establishments, but makes scant attempt to relate to Millennium Place, from which it was intended to be subservient and to cascade riverward. Changes in materials and play of angles appear almost random.

The Market Place, itself a significant place, has recently been given an inappropriate modern makeover by a quango, Durham City Vision, which was established in 2007 and given £5¼ million by ONE NorthEast to regenerate the centre of the city. The driving force was to create a performance space in the Market Place, an action that was seen as essential to increase tourist numbers and thereby revitalise the whole city. The project progressed despite widespread and near-universal opposition from the architectural and planning professions, civic leaders and the public.[4] The equestrian statue was moved from its age-long and logical position and an empty space produced, floored by foreign stone. **(126)** The area for delivery vehicles was removed, resulting in random parking between granite seats ('pods') or in the events space. The omission of kerbing in favour of 'shared space' has proved confusing and dangerous – quite apart from its visual incongruence – such that an array of bollards had to be introduced.

In addition to the three recent major schemes, the reports and recommendations of outside consultants have been disturbing. A common failing among this group, to which the term 'specialist' is given, is their apparent lack of vision beyond their particular specialism: a lack of appreciation of the inter-related nature of the totality that constitutes environment, let alone Durham in particular. At times it is almost as if the canvas of Durham is blank or abstract space in which the modern forces of economics have free play for their brush work or designs.

An associated, non-trivial comment on the language of consultants may also be made at this point. The very consideration of the city's qualities in terms of assets or resources reflects a mindset that evaluates with regard to development, for assets are to be realised, resources to be used or exploited. Cost is the consideration rather than value, returns rather than intrinsic worth. It is literally a world away from 'topophilia', the geographer's neologism to describe human beings' total affective ties with the material environment.

The credence that might be given to outside consultants is tested when, for example, traffic engineers recommend a park-and-walk at Palmer's Close, on the lip of the gorge at the southern tip of the meander. Here, the playing field would be resurfaced for cars and a new high-level footbridge erected over the Wear to the 'under-utilised' bailey.[5] Again, Edinburgh consultants recommended driving a diagonal footpath across Palace Green, aligned directly from the top of Owengate to the north door of the cathedral. The triangular half to the south-east would be grassed; that to the north-west would be given over to the parking of vehicles.[6]

In 2004 leisure consultants put forward recommendations 'to fundamentally transform Durham as a visitor centre'.[7] In their opinion, 'Durham's assets need to be brought to life' – even if this means 'taking liberties' with cherished local treasures. Thus the castle should be 'opened up', and tourist entrepreneurs might be brought in to manage it on behalf of the university; medieval events could be staged on Palace Green; colourful medieval banners could be hung across the ancient bridges to promote attractions on offer. Further, the riverbanks, 'arguably Durham's most under-utilised asset', have potential for water sports, casual sports area, cafés, bandstand, lights, festivals, themed events, and so on. 'Without this [development] Durham's most flexible, fresh and multi-faceted resource will remain ... a waterway.' Such developments would add what was termed 'grooviness', and balance the current 'gravitas' of the peninsula. Visits were recommended to Brighton and Milton Keynes to see 'how it is done'. Doubtless the same consultants would have voted for the entry from the architectural practice in the competition for the city's Millennium Scheme that included an aerial cable car from the railway station to Claypath.

The appearance in 2006 of a tourist open-top, double-decker, hop on, hop off bus was presumably an example of the grooviness that was envisaged. It did not reappear the following season, having been no more successful or appropriate in a small 'walkable' city than the earlier near-disastrous trial of a horse-drawn carriage intended to ferry tourists between the Market Place and Palace Green.

126 The Market Place today.

Tourism, of course, is a major growth industry, and Durham, as a historic city, would be expected to participate – and, of course, benefit by exploiting current under-use of resources. In the late 1980s a joint five-year City-County initiative aimed to attract a 10 per cent annual increase in visitors. Fortunately the goal was not attained. The 2004 consultants' report reawakened hopes. Thus the County Authority's cabinet member for tourism and business commented that ' Durham needs to be in the same league as the historic cities of York, Chester and Bath ... But we draw only a fraction of the visitors who go to these cities.'

Apart from the fact that Durham is a much smaller city, with far fewer 'attractions', one may query whether Durham really would welcome an explosion in visitor numbers, for there are always accompanying disbenefits. Increased toll on physical fabric is the most obvious, but there would also be questions of ambience of historic experience and quality of life in the host community. Would residents really welcome, and visitors enjoy, even a doubling of numbers? For this is a reasonable figure to contemplate if Durham really were to have the likes of York and Bath in its sights. An end scenario might well be the experience when making a pilgrimage to many another World Heritage Site abroad, and finding oneself trying to block out the seething throng in order to imbibe the wonder of the place – and reflecting on the sobriety in Durham. A cautionary view has certainly been put forward by David Lowenthal, international scholar on heritage: 'Durham's appeal rests partly from <u>not</u> being a major tourist destination.'[8] This may sound an elitest comment, but there is no wish to discourage any who would like to visit historic Durham, only to question the pace and nature of proposals recommended by consultants.

When one contemplates many of the schemes recently mooted, the words of another international writer come to mind. 'The risk' of tourism, writes Jokilehto, 'is to substitute the identity of an historic town with that of a tourist centre, which can easily lead to kitsch and be destructive.'[9] If this is but one person's comment, those with responsibility for the future of Durham surely have a duty to heed the Charter on Cultural Tourism prepared by ICOMOS and endorsed by UNESCO: 'It is the respect of the world cultural and natural heritage which must take precedence over any other considerations, however justified these may be from a social, political or economic point of view.'[10]

The vision of the future of the city held by the County Authority may also be questioned. County Hall is located on Aykley Heads Estate, an extensive parkland in the green setting of the city. The contribution of the parkland, with views to and from the cathedral, was recognised in protective policies in the first County Structure Plan of 1981. It was a surprise, therefore, when in 1987 a County Durham Development Company was formed 'to unlock any asset' in its exploitation of the estate. Seven sites for offices and a hotel on the south and east edges, overlooking the city, were duly advertised, and a planning application lodged. It was withdrawn after protests and the threat of a call-in by the Government Office for the North East.

The Authority's attitude to the green belt around the city has also been difficult to comprehend. Thus, in the mid-1990s it was surprising that at the consultation stage in the revision of the Structure Plan there was no reference to a green belt, even though recent advice from central government had added protection of historic towns as an additional reason for their creation. Following an outcry, the subsequent deposit draft did concede a mean, discontinuous area, with Aykley Heads Estate among the excluded sections. It took a green belt campaign and an examination in public (and inspector's decision) to achieve a continuous green belt. Although the east and southern parts of Aykley Heads were included, overall, Durham's green belt was tightly drawn, and is only a quarter of the size of any other historic town.

For two years from 2004 the Authority explored the possibility, made plans and used consultancies for a relief road a mile downriver from the cathedral. It involved a dual carriageway, and crawler lanes, from the A690 down into the Wear Valley, with a new bridge over the river. The area to be traversed is entirely green belt and an Area of High Landscape Value, with patches of ancient woodland, and is on the doorstep of medieval Crook Hall and Kepier Hospital. It would also destroy one of the famous 'long views' for which Durham is famous.

The view was included as an illustration by Thomas Sharp in his 1945 *Plan*. The accompanying comment that the 'tremendous scene ... is a good deal nearer ideal than any real scene has a right to be'[11] is afforded added poignancy when it is remembered that he had recently argued successfully against a coal-fired power station in the same area.

The new road, which of course would have been landscaped and would foster prosperity – the same promises were made for the power station – would surely sum to a negative score on any cost-benefit analysis. Apart from ravage of the landscape, apart from noise, fumes and light pollution, and apart from an admitted increase in fatal and serious accidents, the actual relief in traffic congestion would be minimal. The County Authority's own consultants' estimate was that only one in five vehicles would divert to the new road.

Most recently, in 2010, the County Authority returned to the green belt by proposing that two-thirds of the city's housing in the next plan period should be on the narrowly-delimited green belt land. This proposal flies in the face of central government policy, which states that 'the essential characteristic of Green Belts is their permanence'. The government-appointed inspector at the previous inquiry considered there to be sufficient land for housing at least for the medium term.

The same plan targets the city for disproportionate growth in order to lead regeneration in the whole of the county. In the words of the initial *Core Strategies Issues* document, the city 'needs a critical mass of population, employment and visitors ... to maximise this potential for the benefit of the County'.[12] The county planning officer recently re-emphasised the intention: 'The population is too small to attract many of the facilities we want. Population is really holding Durham back in many respects.'[13]

The recommendations, intentions and policies in recent times, described here, justify the use of 'futures', for there must be an alternative, certainly if the English Heritage definition of conservation is applied, for bigness is of no intrinsic worth or attraction for Durham. Indeed, an integral part of its distinctiveness is that, unlike many an internationally renowned townscape or architectural climax, it is not set in the middle of some large metropolitan area. There is no long traversing of the ordinary before encountering the extraordinary. Bill Bryson is only the most recent to be captivated by the city's compactness and small size – 'a perfect little city'.[14] Planner Thomas Sharp's view was that 'There is no need for Durham to grow large. There is no benefit in it: indeed, there would be injury.'[15]

To resort to the language of economics: any resource is finite. Durham as a resource is infinitely vulnerable, given its size and compact nature, to which reference has just been made. If sustainability means safeguarding the present for future generations, then one has to look beyond one plan period, even one generation or even one lifetime. We are concerned with continuities. The future is a journey, not a terminus: it concerns travelling, not arriving – except to know the place for the first time.

In the management of change, responsible stewardship needs to recognise that not every development constitutes 'progress', not every promise of employment is appropriate. The Kepier power station promised both. The key test of responsible stewardship is whether there will be continuity in change: whether what is proposed will preserve or enrich the quality of Durhamness. If there were half a dozen cities like Durham, perhaps the test could be less stringent. But there is only one Durham, and twenty-first-century 'improvers', not least, might reflect that its unique urban ensemble – a storied place written in memorable townscape – is at the same time a vulnerable entity. After 1,000 years a few generations of 'successful' developments could convert a small city into a metropolis possessing the standard, the normal, the expected. But Durham is not a city of the expected. In this respect, one is reminded of the pessimism in Philip Larkin's poem, 'Going, going', if Durham is substituted for England:

Despite all the land left free,
For the first time I feel somehow
That it isn't going to last
And that will be Durham gone.[15]

Preferable, surely, for resident and visitor, planner and planned, is the vision of T.S. Eliot, again with the same substitution:

Here, the intersection of the timeless moment
Is Durham and nowhere. Never and always.[16]

The future of the past has recently been assured for three precious sites near to the city centre which today contribute to the attractiveness of Durham and which in the past have featured in its historic evolution. Foremost is Crook Hall, a haven of tranquillity just downriver and slightly elevated above the Wear. At its heart is a medieval manor, complete with minstrels' gallery, linked by a Jacobean extension to a three-storey Georgian house. With candles flickering in the hall and wood smoke detectable in the drawing room, it is no surprise to learn that it has its own ghost. The Hall is set in 4 acres of enchanting gardens. Both house and garden have been lovingly restored and cared for by its present and immediate past owners. Notable past owners have included John de Copeland, who captured King David after the Battle of Neville's Cross, and Thomas Billingham, who gave the city its first water supply in the fifteenth century.

Old Durham Gardens, barely a mile upriver, has lost the mid-seventeenth-century manor house of John Heath, but not its formal gardens. Their survival today is attributable to the city council, which acquired them in 1985 and undertook the initial restoration and repair. A Friends organisation has most recently solicitously maintained the site. Historical, archaeological and horticultural research aided the restoration and replanting of herbaceous borders and grafting of old varieties of fruit. Today the restored site, in its tranquil, sylvan location, consists of an upper walled garden, with gazebo, which overlooks terraces, or 'hanging gardens', down to a lower level of orchard garden. Throughout the nineteenth century the site was 'a place of public resort', with summer concerts held in the upper garden. A public house, The Pineapple, arose to serve the visitors. By the first half of the twentieth century the number of drinkers had far exceeded those wishing to listen to music, its licence was lost and the area abandoned until its recent revival.

Flass Vale is a wilderness area extending from just beyond the railway viaduct to the rim of the bowl in which the city sits. Within it is Bower's Mount, a Bronze Age burial ground, which is better remembered as the hillock on which the prior and monks prayed while the Battle of Neville's Cross was raging. The flat floor of the Vale was once the collecting ground of the waters of the Milneburn, which was used to power medieval tanning mills. The Vale was registered as common land in the mid-1970s, and is now recognised as a local nature reserve. The remarkable natural haven, on the very doorstep of the city centre, is today overseen by a Friends organisation.

NOTES

Chapter One

1. Arthur Holmes, *Principles of Physical Geology*, Thomas Nelson & Sons Ltd: London (1944).
2. Pamela Lowther *et al*, 'The city of Durham: an archaeological survey', *Durham Archaeological Journal*, vol. 9 (1993), 27–119.
3. I.A. Richmond *et al*, 'A civilian bath-house of the Roman period at Old Durham', *Archaeological Aeliana*, 22 (1944), 1–26.
4. P.A.G. Clack, *The Book of Durham City*, Barracuda: London (1985), 21.
5. L. Sherley-Price (trans.), *Bede; A History of the English Church and People*, *Penguin*: Harmondsworth (1982).
6. D. Rollason, *Saints and Relics in Anglo-Saxon England*, Basil Blackwell: Oxford (1989).
7. D.W. Rollason (ed.), *Cuthbert, Saint and Patron*, Dean and Chapter: Durham (1987).
8. Symeon of Durham (trans. J. Stephenson), *A History of the Church of Durham,* Llanerch Enterprises, Lampeter (1988).
9. J.T. Fowler, *Rites of Durham*, Surtees Society, No. 107 (1903).
10. Sir Walter Scott, 'Marmion: a tale of Flodden Field', *The Poetical Works of Sir Walter Scott, Bart.,* George Routledge: London (n.d.), 120.
11. Eric Cambridge, 'Archaelogy and the cult of St Oswald in Pre-Conquest Northumbria', in E. Cambridge and C. Stancliffe (eds), *Oswald: Northumbrian King to European Saint,* Paul Watkins: Stamford (1995), 128–63.

Chapter Two

1. Symeon, *op. cit.*, 70.
2. *Ibid.*, 75.
3. W.M. Aird, 'An absent friend: the career of Bishop William of St Calais', in D. Rollason, M. Harvey, M. Prestwich (eds), *Anglo-Norman Durham: 1093–1193*, Boydell Press, Woodbridge (1993), 283–98.

4. Alan Piper, 'The cathedral and its monastic community', in Douglas Pocock (ed.), *St Cuthbert and Durham Cathedral: A Celebration*, City of Durham Trust, Durham (1993), 95.

5. D. Rollason, 'Northumbria: a failed European kingdom', in R. Colls (ed.), *Northumbria History and Identity 547–2000*, Phillimore, Chichester (2007), 11.

6. Malcolm Thurlby, 'The roles of the patron and the master mason in the first design of the Romanesque cathedral of Durham', in D. Rollason, M. Harvey, M. Prestwich (eds), *op. cit.*, 161–84. Malcolm Thurlby, 'The building of the cathedral: the Romanesque and Early Gothic Fabric' in Douglas Pocock (ed.), *op. cit.*, 15–35. I. Curry, 'Aspects of the Anglo-Norman design of Durham cathedral', *Archaeologia Aeliana* (1987), 31–48.

7. W. St J. Hope, 'Recent discoveries in the cloister of Durham abbey', *Proceedings of the Society of Antiquities,* 22 (1909), 417–24.

8. John Field, *Durham Cathedral: Light of the North,* Third Millennium Publishing, London (2006), 42.

9. J.O. Prestwich, 'The career of Ranulf Flambard' in D. Rolason, M. Harvey, M. Prestwich (eds), *op. cit.*, 299–310.

10. C.J. Stranks, *This Sumptuous Church*, SPCK, London (1973), 9–11.

11. Martin Roberts, *Durham: 1000 Years of History*, Tempus Publishing Ltd, Stroud (2003), 66.

12. M. Leyland, 'The origins and development of Durham castle', in D. Rollason, M. Harvey, M. Prestwich (eds), *op. cit.*, 407–24.

13. G.A.L. Johnson and K. Dunham, 'The stones of Durham Cathedral: a preliminary note', *Transactions, Durham & Northumberland Architectural & Archaeological Society,* 6 (1982), 53.

14. David Park, 'The interior decoration of the cathedral', in Douglas Pocock (ed.), *op. cit.*, 57–67.

15. David Park, 'The wall paintings in the Galilee Chapel of Durham Cathedral', *Friends of Durham Cathedral Annual Report,* 57 (1990), 21–34.

16. Jane Geddes, 'The sanctuary ring of Durham Cathedral', *Archaeologia*, 107 (1982), 127.

17. G.V. Scammell, *Hugh du Puiset*, Cambridge University Press , Cambridge (1956), 92.

18. R. Norris, 'The cathedral and its early books', in D. Pocock (ed.), *op. cit.*, 103–9.

19. Margaret Bonney, *Lordship and the Urban Community: Durham and its Overlords 1250–1540*, Cambridge University Press, Cambridge (1990), 27-31.

20. R. Hamer, *A Choice of Anglo-Saxon Verse*, Faber & Faber, London (1970), 33.

21. R.J. Dickinson, 'A description of Durham by Lawrence the monk', in R.J. Dickinson and J. Middlemass (eds), *City of Durham 1179-1979*, Guinness & Rawson, Newcastle (1979), 12.

Chapter Three

1. Fowler, *op. cit.*, 10–12.
2. R.C. Norris, 'The cathedral glass', *Friends of Durham Cathedral Annual Report* 51 (1984), 14–20. R.C. Norris, *The Stained Glass in Durham Cathedral*, Durham, Dean and Chapter of Durham (1984).
3. Shanks, *op. cit.*, 27.
4. Fowler, *op. cit.*, 56–7.
5. Brian Cheesman, 'South Street: topography, tenure and occupation, part 2', *Durham County Local History Society Bulletin*, 58 (1998), 3–24.
6. Bonney, *op. cit.*, 46.
7. Martin Roberts, *op. cit.*, 107–12.
8. Bonney, *op. cit.*, 280.
9. *Ibid.*, 232–3.
10. Alexander Grant, 'Disaster at Neville's Cross: the Scottish point of view', in D. Rollason and M. Prestwich (eds), *The Battle of Neville's Cross 1346*, Shaun Tyas, Stamford (1998), 35.
11. Martin Roberts, 'Neville's Cross: a suggested reconstruction', in D. Rollason and M. Prestwich (eds), *op. cit.*, 102–11.

Chapter Four

1. Geoffrey Moorhead, *The Last Office*, Weidenfield & Nicolson, London (2008), 35.
2. G.M. Trevelyan, *History of England*, Longmans, Green & Co., London (1952), 297.
3. Shanks, *op. cit.*, 42.
4. Fowler, *op. cit.*, 60.
5. William Page (ed.), *The Victoria History of the Counties of England: A History of Durham*, Dawsons, London (1968), vol. 3, 29.
6. Shanks, *op. cit.*, 50.
7. Francis F. Johnson, *Historic Staircases in Durham City*, City of Durham Trust, Durham (1970), 14–16, 19–20.
8. Margot Johnson (ed.), 'John Cosin: an introduction to his life and work', in Margot Johnson, *John Cosin: From Priest to Prince Bishop*, Turnstone Ventures, Durham (1997), 47.
9. J.D.T. Hall, 'Cosin's library', in Margot Johnson (ed.), *op. cit.*, 94.
10. Arthur Bryant, *Samuel Pepys: The Years of Peril*, Cambridge University Press, Cambridge (1935), 381.
11. J. Oates, 'Durham and the Jacobite revolution of 1715', *Durham County Local History Society Bulletin*, 66 (2003), 27.
12. C. Morris (ed.), *The Journeys of Celia Fiennes*, Gresset, London (1949) 214.

13. C.W. Gibby, 'Durham city: historical survey', in John C. Dewdney (ed.), *Durham County and City with Teesside,* Hindson Reid Jordison, Newcastle upon Tyne (1970), 514.

14. Alan Heesom, *Durham City and its M.P.s 1678–1992*, Durham County Local History Society, Durham (1992), 20.

15. Quoted in C.E. Whiting, *The University of Durham 1832–1932*, Sheldon Press, London (1932), 18.

16. *Extracts from Leland's 'Itinerary' relating to Durham,* Nicholson, South Shields (n.d.), 5–6.

17. William Camden (trans. Gough), 'Bishoprick of Durham' in *Britain, or a Chorographical Description of the most flourishing Kingdom, England, Scotland and Ireland*, London (1806), 351..

18. Robert Hegg, *The Legend of Saint Cuthbert, or the Histories of his Churches*, George Smith, Darlington (1777), 22.

19. Quoted in Douglas Pocock and Roy Gazzard, *Durham: Portrait of a Cathedral City*, City of Durham Trust and University of Durham, Durham (1983), 26.

20. M. Roberts, 'The prospect of Durham from the south-east. A late-seventeenth century panorama of the city', *Durham County Local History Society Bulletin*, 67 (2003), 7–27.

Chapter Five

1. Shanks, *op. cit.*, 71.

2. E. Hughes (ed.), *Letters of Dean Spencer Cowper* (1950), 61.

3. James Murray, *The Travels of Imagination: A True Journey from Newcastle to London*, W. Fordyce, Newcastle (1828), 34.

4. Ian Curry, *Sense and Sensitivity: Durham Cathedral and its Architects*, Durham, Durham Cathedral (1985), 7–16.

5. Rosalind Billingham, 'The artists' response: images of Durham Cathedral from c.1780', in Douglas Pocock (ed.), *Durham Cathedral: A Celebration*, City of Durham Trust, Durham (1993), 74–94.

6. T. Gray, 'Letter to Rev. Mr Brown, 24th July 1753', in P. Toynbee and L. Whibley, *Correspondence of Thomas Gray*, Oxford University Press, Oxford (1935), vol. 1, 379–80.

7. M.W. Thompson (ed.), *The Journeys of Sir Richard Colt Hoare through England and Wales 1793–1810*, Alan Sutton, Gloucester (1983), 144.

8. Martin Roberts (2003), *op. cit.*, 146–8.

9. C. Morris (ed.), *op. cit.*, 213.

10. P. Rogers (ed.), *Daniel Defoe: A Tour through the Whole Kingdom of Great Britain*, Penguin, Harmondsworth (1971), 533.

11. I.M. Knapp (ed.), *Tobias Smollett: The Expedition of Humphrey Clinker*, Oxford University Press, Oxford (1966), 187.

12. Quoted in Shanks, *op. cit.*, 75.
13. Francis F. Johnson, *Historic Staircases in Durham City*, City of Durham Trust, Durham (1970), 39–41.
14. Walter Shea, *Carpet Making in Durham City*, City, Durham County Council, Durham (1984), 32–9.
15. Ivor Atkinson and Roger Norris, 'The account of the Messrs Salvin's cotton mill', *Transactions of the Architectural and Archaeological Society of Durham & Northumberland,* 6 (1952), 1–3.
16. C. Morris (ed.), *op. cit.*, 213.

Chapter Six

1. M.W. Thompson (ed.), *The Journeys of Sir William Colt Hoare through Wales and England 1793–1810*, Alan Sutton, Gloucester (1983), 143–44.
2. Sir Walter Scott, *op. cit.*, 120.
3. Alan Heesom, 'The Duke of Wellington's visit to the North East of England, September–October 1827', *Durham County Local History Society*, 60 (1999), 14.
4. Alan Heesom, ' Who thought of the idea of the University of Durham?' *Durham County Local History Society*, 29 (1982), 15.
5. Alan Heesom, *ibid.*, 16.
6. J.H. Crosby, *Ignatius Bonomi of Durham, Architect*, City of Durham Trust, Durham (1987).
7. Quoted in D. Butler, 'Street lighting in Durham City before the advent of Gas', *Durham County Local History Society*, 38 (1987), 27.
8. Alan Heesom (1992), *op. cit.*, 29–32.
9. Robert Surtees, *The History and Antiquities of the County Palatine of Durham*, London (1840), vol. IV, 4.

Chapter Seven

1. Alan Maitland, *Durham City and the Railway Age*, Historical Association and University of Durham (1995), 22–3.
2. *Durham Advertiser*, September 1842, quoted in Alan Maitland, *op. cit.*, 5.
3. G.W.E. Russell (ed.), *Letters of Matthew Arnold*, Macmillan, London (1895), vol.1, 154.
4. Philip A. Grant, 'The Coalmines of Durham City', *Occasional Publication*, Dept of Geography, University of Durham, No. 2 (1973), 11.
5. June Crosby, *op. cit.*, 85.
6. P.B. Attewell and R.K. Taylor, 'Foundation engineering; some geotechnical considerations', in John C. Dewdney (ed.), *Durham County and City with Teesside*, British Association, Durham (1970), facing 92, 102.

7. David Temple, *The Big Meeting: A History of the Durham Miners' Gala,* TUPS Books in conjunction with Durham Mineworkers' Union, Washington (2011).

8. C.C.H., 'Durham', *The Builder*, 31 March 1866, 228.

9. Walter Shea, *op. cit.*, 32–81.

10. Quoted in Walter Shea, *op. cit.*, 78–9.

11. J. H. Crosby, *op. cit.*

12. Alan Maitland, *op. cit.*, 16.

13. C.E. Whiting, *The University of Durham, 1832–1932*, Sheldon Press, London, (1932), 139.

14. Quoted in D. Butler, '"The chief ornament of his native city": William Henderson and the building of Durham's town hall', *Durham County Local History Society*, 75 (2010), 39.

15. Quoted in Nikolaus Pevsner, revised Elizabeth Williamson, *The Buildings of England: County Durham*, Penguin, Harmondsworth (1983), 222.

16 C.C.H., *The Builder, op. cit.*, 228.

17. John E. McCutcheon, *Troubled Seams: A Durham County Mining Narrative of the 19th Century*, J. Greenwood & Sons, Seaham (1955); also *Durham County Advertiser,* 2 September 1955.

18. Eric Halladay, *Rowing in England: A Social History: The Amateur Debate*, Manchester University Press, Manchester (1990).

19. Matthew E. Frisby, 'The Scott choir screen', *Friends of Durham Cathedral Annual Report*, 63 (1996), 30.

20. *Ibid.*, 31.

Chapter Eight

1. D.J. Butler, 'Durham City, its boundaries and population, 1801–1974', *Durham Local History Society*, 59 (1998), 3–29.

2. *Durham Advertiser,* 14 July 1983.

3. *Durham University Journal*, 26 (June 1929), 29.

4. Nigel Watson, *The Durham Difference: The story of Durham University*, James & James, London (2007), 49.

5. Owen Chadwick, *Michael Ramsey: A Life*, Clarendon, Oxford (1990).

6. *Durham County Advertiser*, 1 September 1933.

7. David Williams, *Cinema in a Cathedral City, 1896–2003*, Mercia, Wakefield (2004).

8. Thomas Sharp, 'The North-East – Hills and Hells', in C. William-Ellis (ed.), *Britain and the Beast,* J.M. Dent & Sons, London, 141–59.

9. Thomas Sharp, *Cathedral City: A Plan for Durham City*, Architectural Press, London, 1945.

10. *Ibid.*, 15, 19, 32.

11. *Ibid.*, 45.

12. *Durham County Advertiser*, 1 September 1927.

13. Interview with Dr Thomas Sharp, *Northern Architect*, 47 (1969), 86.

14. *The Times*, 14 July 1944.

Chapter Nine

1. Nikolaus Pevsner, *The Buildings of England: County Durham*, Penguin, Harmondsworth (1953), 123.

2. Ian Nairn, 'Stop press', *Architectural Review*, 143 (1968), 403.

3. Thomas Sharp (1969), *op. cit.*, 89.

4. A. Clifton-Taylor, 'Durham', *Another Six Towns*, Alastair Press, Bury St Edmunds (1989).

5. Anon., 'Durham University Development Plan 1969', *Northern Architect*, 50 (1970), 151.

6. William Whitfield and Brian Hackett, *University of Durham Development Plan 1969: Draft Written Statement*, Durham (1969), 8.

7. Patrick Nuttgens, quoted in Peter Pace, *The Architecture of George Pace*, B.T. Batsford, London (1990), 200.

8. R.W. Paine, 'Architecture at the Royal Academy', *The Builder*, 12 May 1963.

9. Douglass Wise, quoted in Martin Roberts, *op. cit.*, 169.

10. J.H. Robinson and D. Neave, *Francis Johnson, Architect: A Classical Statement*, Oblong, Otley (2001), 94.

Chapter Ten

1. Anon., 'The world's best buildings', part 1, *Illustrated London News* (May 1984), 50–7.

2. N. Pevsner, *Outline of European Architecture*, Penguin, Harmondsworth (1963), 66.

3. N. Pevsner (revised by E. Williamson), *op. cit.*, 159–60.

4. Douglas Pocock, 'The view from Prebends' Bridge', in Douglas Pocock (ed.), *op. cit.* (1999), 71–9.

Chapter Eleven

1. Douglas Pocock (1999), *op. cit.*, 6–12.

2. R. Stewart (ed.), *The English Notebooks by Nathaniel Hawthorne*, Oxford University Press (1941), 543.

3. C.S. Lewis, (ed.) Walter Hooper, *Other Worlds: Essays and Stories*, Geoffrey Bles, London (1966), 42.

4. A.N. Wilson, *C.S. Lewis: A Biography*, Harper Perennial, London (2005), 197.

5. Douglas Pocock, *In the Steps of the Masters: Durham in Paintings,* City of Durham Trust, Durham (2010).
6. Alec Clifton-Taylor, *op. cit.*, 180.
7. Thomas Sharp in C. Williams-Ellis (ed), *op. cit.,* 150.
8. J. B. Priestley, *English Journey*, Penguin, Harmondsworth (1977), 302.
9. Sid Chaplin, *A Tree with Rosy Apples*, Frank Graham, Newcastle (1972), 84.

Chapter Twelve

1. Douglas Pocock, *The Futures of Durham*, City of Durham Trust, Durham (2006)
2. English Heritage, *Conservation Principles: Policies and Guidance for the Sustainable Management of the Historic Environment* (2008), 71.
3. Douglas Pocock, *The Unmaking of Durham's Historic Market Place,* City of Durham Trust, Durham (2010).
4. Buchanan & Partners, *Durham City Travel Study: Final Report,* Edinburgh (1997).
5. Shepherd, Epstein, Hunter, *Durham University Master Plan and Development Framework,* Edinburgh (2006).
6. The Chambers/Donaldson, *Planning for the Future of the City of Durham: The New Retail and Leisure Offer*, London (2004).
7. D. Lowenthal, 'Durham: Perils and Promises of a Heritage', public lecture in Durham (1988).
8. J. Jokilehto, *A History of Architectural Conservation*, Butterworth-Heinemann, London (1988).
9. ICOMOS, *Charter on Cultural Tourism,* International Council on Monuments and Sites, Paris (1976).
10. Thomas Sharp (1945), *op. cit.*, 88.
11. Durham County Council, *Planning the Future of County Durham: Core Strategy Issues and Options Paper*, Durham, June 2010, 31.
12. Stuart Timmiss, County Planning Officer, *Durham Times*, 6 August 2010.
13. Bill Bryson, *Notes from a Small Island*, Black Swan, London (1996), 294.
14. Thomas Sharp (1945), *op. cit.*, 28.
15. Philip Larkin, *Collected Poems*, Faber & Faber Ltd, London (1988).
16. T.S. Eliot, *Collected Poems*, Faber & Faber Ltd, London (1963).

SELECT BIBLIOGRAPHY

Andrews, Patricia R., *Durham Cathedral: Artists and Images*, Durham County Council, Durham (1993)

Billings, R.W., *Illustrations of the Architectural Antiquities of the County of Durham* (1846, facsimile reprint 1974)

Bonner, G., Rollason, D., Stancliffe, C. (eds), *St Cuthbert, His Cult and Community to AD 1200*, Boydell, Woodbridge (1989)

Bonny, Margaret, *Lordship and the Urban Community: Durham and its Overlords 1250–1540*, Cambridge University Press, Cambridge (1990)

Brickstock, R.J., *Durham Castle: Fortress, Palace, College*, Jeremy Mills, Huddersfield (2007)

Chadwick, Owen, *Hensley Henson and the Durham Miners,* Dean & Chapter, Durham (1983)

Chadwick, Owen, *Lord Ramsey: A Life*, Clarendon, Oxford (1990)

Clark, P.A.G. (ed.), *The Book of Durham City*, Barracuda, Buckingham (1985)

Colls, R. (ed.), *Northumbria History and Identity 547–2000*, Phillimore, Chichester (2007)

Crosby, J.H., *Ignatius Bonomi of Durham*, City of Durham Trust, Durham (1987)

Dewdney, J.C. (ed.), *Durham County and City with Teesside*, British Association, Durham (1970)

Martin Dufferwiel, *Durham: A Thousand Years of History and Images*, Mainstream Publishing, London (1996)

Emery, Norman, *Monks and Masons: The Archaeology of Durham Cathedral*, University of Durham (n.d.)

Field, John, *Durham Cathedral: Light of the North*, Third Millennium Publishing, London (2006)

Fowler, J.T., *Rites of Durham*, Surtees Society, 107 (1903)

Grant, Philip A., *The Coalmines of Durham City*, Occasional Publication, Department of Geography, University of Durham, 2 (1973)

Heesom, Alan, *Durham City and its MPs 1678–1992*, Durham County Local History Society (1992)

Hutchinson, William, *The History and Antiquities of the County Palatine of Durham*, S. Hodgson, Newcastle, 3 vols (1785–94)

Johnson, Francis F., *Historic Staircases in Durham City*, City of Durham Trust, Durham (1970)

Johnson, Margot (ed.), *John Cosin: From Priest to Prince Bishop*, Turnstone Ventures, Durham (1997)

Garside, W.R., *The Durham Miners 1919–1960*, Allen & Unwin, London (1971)

Halladay, Eric, *Rowing in England: A Social History: The Amateur Debate*, Manchester University Press, Manchester (1990)

Maitland, Alan, *Durham City and the Railway Age*, Historical Association and University of Durham (1995)

Moorhead, Geoffrey, *The Last Office*, Weidenfeld & Nicolson, London (1995)

Norris, Roger, *The Stained Glass in Durham Cathedral*, Dean & Chapter, Durham, (1984)

Page, William (ed.), *The Victoria County History of the Counties of England: A History of Durham*, Dawsons, London, London, vol. 3 (1968)

Pevsner, Nikolaus (revised Williamson, Elizabeth), *The Buildings of England: County Durham*, Penguin, Harmondsworth (1983)

Pocock, Douglas, *Durham: Essays on Sense of Place*, City of Durham Trust, Durham (1999)

Pocock, Douglas, *The Futures of Durham*, City of Durham Trust, Durham (2006)

Pocock, Douglas, *The Unmaking of Durham's Historic Market Place*, City of Durham Trust, Durham (2010)

Pocock, Douglas, *In the Steps of the Masters: Durham in Paintings*, City of Durham Trust, Durham (2010)

Pocock, Douglas (ed.), *St Cuthbert and Durham Cathedral: A Celebration*, City of Durham Trust, Durham (1993)

Pocock, D. and Norris, R., *A History of County Durham*, Phillimore, Chichester (1990)

Proud, Keith, *Durham City*, Phillimore, Chichester (1992)

Proud, Keith, *The Prince Bishops of Durham*, Keybar (1990)

Roberts, Martin, *Durham: 1000 Years of History*, Tempus Publishing, Stroud (2006)

Rollason, D.W. (ed.), *Cuthbert: Saint and Patron*, Dean & Chapter, Durham (1987)

Rollason, David, Harvey, Margaret, Prestwich, Michael (eds), *Anglo-Norman Durham: 1093–1193*, Boydell Press, Woodbridge (1993)

Rollason, David, Prestwich, Michael (eds), *The Battle of Neville's Cross*, Shaun Press (1998)

Shanks, C.J., *This Sumptuous Church*, SPCK, London (1984)

Sharp, Thomas, *Cathedral City: A Plan for Durham City*, Architectural Press, London (1945)

Shea, Walter, *Carpet Making in Durham*, Durham County Council, Durham (1984)

Stephenson, J. (trans.), *Bede: A History of the English Church and People*, Penguin, Harmondsworth (1988)

Surtees, Robert, *The History and Antiquities of the County Palatine of Durham*, 4 vols, London (1816-40)

Temple, David, *The Big Meeting: A History of the Durham Miners' Gala*, TUBS Books and Durham Miners' Association, Washington (2011)

Watson, Nigel, *The Durham Difference: The Story of Durham University*, James & James, London (2007)

Whitfield, William, Hackett, Brian, *University of Durham Development Plan 1969, Draft Written Statement*, University of Durham, Durham (1969)

Whiting, C.E., *The University of Durham 1832–1932*, Sheldon Press, London (1932)

Williams, David, *Cinema in a Cathedral City, 1896–2003*, Mercia, Wakefield (2004)

INDEX